T237 Unit 7
Technology: a second level course

The Open
University

ENVIRONMENTAL
•CONTROL • AND•
PUBLIC • HEALTH •

W A T E R

Unit 7
Water supply
and sewage treatment

PREPARED BY THE COURSE TEAM

T237 Environmental control and public health: Course Team

Professor Andrew Porteous	Course Team Chairman	Caryl Hunter-Brown	Liaison Librarian
Judith Anderson	Course Manager	Dr Tony Jolly	BBC
Prof. Keith Attenborough	Technology	Dr Andrew Millington	BBC
Cameron Balbirnie	BBC	Dr Suresh Nesaratnam	Technology
Dr Rod Barratt	Technology	Dr John Newbury	Technology Staff Tutor
Lesley Booth	Course Secretary	Dr Brian Price	Unit writing consultant
Dr Keith Cavanagh	Project Officer	Janice Robertson	Editor
Dr David Cooke	Technology Staff Tutor	Ian Spratley	BBC
Sue Dobson	Graphic Artist	Doreen Tucker	Text Processing Compositor
Pamela Furniss	Technology	Bob Walters	BBC
Morine Gordon	Course Secretary	Dr David Yeoman	Unit writing consultant
Caroline Hailey	Graphic Designer		

In addition, the Course Team wishes to thank the following for reviewing this material (1992 designations):

External Assessor	Professor Jacob Lewin, Lewin Fryer & Partners, Consulting Engineers
Statistics and epidemiology:	Elizabeth Overton, Public Health Laboratory Services
Wastes:	Colin Palmer, Principal Assistant County Surveyor, Suffolk County Council; John Birch, Managing Director (designate), Lincwaste
Air:	Dr Jimi Irwin, Warren Spring Laboratory

Contents of the course

This text has been printed on Savannah Natural Art™: at least 60% of the fibre used in the production of this paper is bagasse (fibrous residue of sugarcane, a waste byproduct of sugar processing) and the balance is softwood fibre which has undergone an oxygen bleaching process.

The Open University, Walton Hall, Milton Keynes, MK7 6AA.

First published 1993. Second edition 1995. Reprinted with amendments 1997.

Edited, designed and typeset by the Open University.

Printed in the United Kingdom by Hobbs the Printers, Brunel Road, Totton, Hampshire SO40 3YS.

This text forms part of an Open University Second Level Course. If you would like a copy of *Studying with the Open University*, please write to Course Enquiries Data Service, PO Box 625, Dane Road, Milton Keynes, MK1 1TY, United Kingdom. If you have not already enrolled on the course and would like to buy this or other Open University material, please write to Open University Worldwide, The Open University, Walton Hall, Milton Keynes, MK7 6AA, United Kingdom.

ISBN 0 7492 7298 8

Edition 2.2

17244C/t237u7i2.2

Unit 7
Water supply and sewage treatment

Contents

not examined → 5.9.3

not examined → 5.9.9
5.9.10
5.9.11

AIMS AND OBJECTIVES

The aims of this unit are:

1   to give an introduction to the subject of water supply and demand, and

2   to give an overview of the processes of water and sewage treatment.

After studying this unit, including its relevant television broadcasts, and after carrying out the associated home experiments and assignments, you should be able to:

1   Explain in your own words the following terms and concepts (terms in bold italics are defined in Porteous, 1992):

activated carbon

activated sludge process

activated sludge rate constant

advanced water treatment

aeration/aeration efficiency

alternating double filtration

anaerobic digestion

aquifer/ground water

biological filter

biological oxidation

chemical conditioning of sludge

chloramines

coagulation and *flocculation*

combined/separate sewerage system

comminution

contact stabilisation

Deep Shaft™ process

desalination

disinfection

dry weather flow

electrodialysis

evaporation/evapotranspiration

flotation

fluoridation

food-to-microorganism (F/M) ratio

gravity sewer

grit

humus

hydrological cycle

infiltration water

ion exchange

microstraining

mixed liquor/MLSS

multistage flash distillation

nitrification/denitrification

organic loading rate

oxidation ditch

ozonation

package treatment plant

per capita water consumption

percolation

plumbo-solvency

polyelectrolyte

precipitation

preliminary/primary/secondary/ tertiary treatment of sewage

pure oxygen process

rapid gravity filter

reed beds

retention time

reverse osmosis

rising main

rotating biological contactor

screening

sedimentation

self-cleansing velocity

septic tank

service reservoir

slow sand filter

sludge

sludge age

sludge bulking

sludge volume index

soakaway

solar still

storm overflow

transmission/distribution mains

waste stabilisation ponds

water table

10/10/10 standard

2   Identify the principal demands for water in society. [SAQs 1, 7]

3   Describe methods by which water usage and leakage may be minimised. [SAQ 2]

4   Describe the operation and mechanisms of the hydrological cycle. [SAQs 3–6]

5   Explain the function of transmission mains, ring mains, service reservoirs and water towers, and discuss the merits and disadvantages of different types of piping materials. [SAQs 7, 8]

6   Explain the mode by which potable water is produced through the processes of screening, microstraining, aeration, coagulation and flocculation, sedimentation, flotation, filtration, and disinfection. [SAQs 9–11, 14]

7   Compare slow sand filtration with rapid sand filtration. [SAQ 12]

8   Summarise the advantages and disadvantages of chlorine and ozone in the disinfection of water. [SAQ 13]

9   List the main methods for the removal of nitrates from water. [SAQ 14]

10   Calculate the amount of fluoride compound required to achieve the requisite fluoride level in drinking water. [SAQ 15]

11   Describe the major desalination processes used to produce potable water from saline or brackish sources. [SAQ 16]

12   List the advantages of gravity sewers. [SAQs 17, 18]

13   Describe the process operations used in treating sewage to the 30/20 standard. [SAQs 19–22, 27, 28, 30, 31]

14   Describe and explain the role of storm overflows and storm tanks. [SAQ 21]

15   Define and distinguish between low rate and high rate biological filters, including the relevant characteristics of different filter media. [SAQ 23]

16   Carry out simple design calculations related to biological filter and activated sludge systems. [SAQs 24–26]

17   List the advantages and disadvantages of the activated sludge process compared with biological filters. [SAQ 27]

18   Give examples of variants of the biological oxidation system for treating effluents and indicate the type of effluent or situation for which each type would be most appropriate. [SAQ 28]

19   Give examples of tertiary treatment processes to reduce suspended solids content (and with it its associated BOD), and the level of ammonia, nitrates or phosphates in a secondary-treated effluent. [SAQ 29]

20   List the sources and characteristics of sewage sludge and describe the various methods by which it may be disposed of. [SAQs 32–35]

21   Describe the various pretreatment processes that may have to be applied to industrial effluents to render them suitable for discharge to sewers for treatment at a domestic sewage treatment plant. [SAQ 36]

1   WATER USAGE

1.1   Introduction

Water is a basic necessity. Figure 1 illustrates some of the more common uses of water in a community.

People take water from lakes, reservoirs, rivers or underground sources, and use and reuse it for a variety of purposes before returning it to watercourses or to the atmosphere. Most of the water used for irrigating crops is returned mainly through drainage and evaporation.

TMA 02 Q1

In other cases, the returned water, although still in the liquid state, may be polluted, sometimes grossly. Some of the water used for cooling purposes in power stations or in industry is evaporated, but most of it is returned relatively near to the point at which it was withdrawn. For instance, of the cooling water used in electricity generation, about 2% is lost by evaporation and 98% is discharged at a temperature some 5–6 °C higher than ambient. By the time it reaches the sea, some of the water in a river may have been used again and again, as illustrated in Figure 1.

1.2   Main uses of water in the UK

TMA

In the UK, usage of water can be classified into five main groups:

1   *Public water supplies*. Of the total water supplied by water companies and public authorities some two-thirds is for *domestic* use and the remaining one-third is for industry. However, a proportion of the water used by industry is for domestic purposes in the factory, such as lavatory flushing, ablutions, cleaning and canteen use, the remainder being used for manufacturing processes and as boiler feed water.

2   *Industry.* For certain processes, industry uses large amounts of water both as a coolant and as a medium for conveying substances, such as cellulose fibres in papermaking, crushed rock in ore preparation and so on. This is obtained by

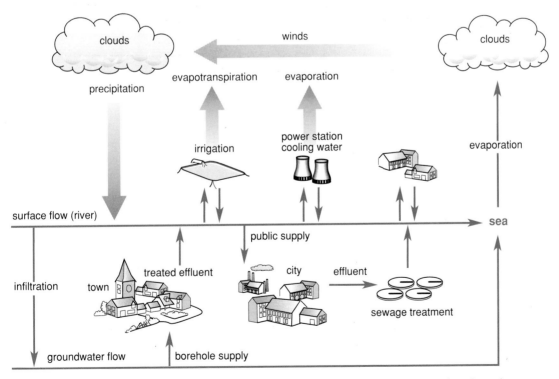

Figure 1   *Simplified diagram to illustrate how water is abstracted from the natural cycle and returned to it after use and reuse.*

direct abstraction. Occasionally, when a high standard of water is needed, direct abstraction is followed by special treatment, but usually such water is obtained from public supplies.

3   *Electricity.* In addition to water used for domestic and industrial processes, the electricity generating companies use large quantities of water, mainly for cooling. Quality requirements are minimal and supplies are always obtained by direct abstraction either from rivers, lakes, estuaries or the sea.

4   *Agriculture.* In the UK, water used by agriculture forms only a minor proportion of the total consumption. Part is used for irrigation, especially in the eastern counties, and the remainder for cattle watering, dairy cleaning and other general purposes.

5   *Waterspace and amenity.* The provision of adequate water space for water-based sports and other activities is of growing importance and we already see reservoirs being built and canals and rivers being improved for recreational and amenity purposes alone.

Estimates of consumption for the first four groups are available from water abstraction figures tabulated by the Department of the Environment. The figures for 1990 are shown in Table 1.

Table 1   *Water abstracted in England and Wales in 1990 for various uses*

Use	Ml d^{-1}	%
Public water supply (used in domestic and industrial premises)	18 336	52.02
Electricity generating companies	12 612	35.78
Industry (excluding water power, saline and tidal abstractions)	3795	10.77
Agriculture (cattle watering, dairy cleaning, fish farming, water cress production, etc.)	129	0.36
Spray irrigation	378	1.07
Total	35 250	100

Source: Department of the Environment (1991) *Digest of Environmental Protection and Water Statistics*, 14, HMSO, London.

As can be seen, public water supplies accounted for some 52% of the total water abstracted. The next biggest use of water was in electricity generating, followed by use in other industries. Spray irrigation, while having a fairly low demand, may have a significant impact on available resources as it tends to be used most during periods of hot dry weather when water resources may already be stretched. Almost all the water used in this way is lost to the atmosphere or ground, unlike water abstracted for other uses which is usually treated and returned to rivers, thus becoming available for use again. The proportions of water supply devoted to these domestic and industrial uses vary appreciably throughout the UK. For instance, in many rural or coastal communities, the industrial element is very small. Elsewhere it may form the major part, as, for example, in the heavily industrialised Teesside region in the north-east of England.

1.3   Per capita consumption

The per capita consumption of water is the amount of water supplied divided by the resident population. If only the domestic element is considered, it is known as the domestic per capita consumption. For Table 1, if we assume that two-thirds (0.67) of the public water supply is used in domestic premises, the domestic per capita water consumption for England and Wales (1990 population, 50.72 million) is

$$\frac{18\,336 \times 10^6 \times 0.67 \text{ l d}^{-1}}{50.72 \times 10^6 \text{ persons}} = 242.21 \text{ l person}^{-1} \text{ d}^{-1}$$

The total per capita water consumption is based on the total quantity of water used in the public water supply (i.e. covering domestic *and* industrial premises).

18 336 ML = 18·336 × 10⁶ L

$$\frac{18\,336 \times 10^{6}\,l}{50.72 \times 10^{6}\,persons} = 361.51\,l\ persons^{-1}\,d^{-1}$$

SAQ 1

Using the figures given in Table 1, calculate the total per capita water consumption in 1990 in England and Wales.

The Water Services Association has published figures for water usage in households. It estimates that in 1991 the average household consumption in England and Wales was 140 l person⁻¹ d⁻¹, made up of the components shown in Table 2.

The figure of 140 l person⁻¹ d⁻¹ is vastly different from the calculated domestic per capita consumption of 242 l person⁻¹ d⁻¹. The difference could be due to major uses of water outside the home such as in swimming pools, road cleaning, etc.

Table 2 *Use of water in the home*

Use	Litres per person per day	% total usage
Toilet flushing	44.8	32
Bathing and showering	23.8	17
Clothes washing	16.8	12
Outside use (gardening, car washing, etc.)	4.2	3
Dishwashing	1.4	1
Miscellaneous (drinking, cooking, leakage, etc.)	49.0	35
Total	140	100

Source: Water Services Association (1991) *Waterfacts*, Water Services Association, London.

In one of the home experiments you will be measuring the rainfall that your home receives, and you will use this data to calculate the proportion of your daily needs that rainfall could satisfy. If you have a metered water supply, calculation of your average daily usage will be easy (since your average water consumption can be ascertained from the figures in your water bill). If your water supply is not metered you will have to make an estimate on the lines of that given in Table 2.

1.4 Water losses

In every distribution system there is some loss of water due mainly to individual joints and glands leaking quantities that are not easily detectable. Large leaks are noticed more quickly, especially if surveys for the detection of leaks are made at regular intervals. In addition, there is usually some apparent loss at meters due to inaccurate registering, but it is not easy to tell precisely what these losses are. Losses can be reduced by using a pressure in the mains which is just enough for efficient supply. Excess water pressure is likely to exacerbate leakage.

In the UK, most industrial supplies and some household supplies are metered and the consumers are charged on the basis of the quantity used. In areas where metering is total, the leakage can be estimated by deducting the amount used by the consumers from the total supplied to the distribution system. In areas where only industrial usage is metered, the probable loss is estimated by measuring demand at night when domestic consumption is at its lowest. Leakage occurs mainly due to pipes fracturing with age or vibration from heavy traffic overhead.

Metering the individual consumer's supply and billing at established meter rates prevents wastage of water by users and tends to reduce actual water usage. The wastage and unaccounted-for water in metered systems ranges from 10% to 15% of the total water entering the distribution system. The average loss on the water companies' side of the meter is about 12% (1996). The corresponding rate in unmetered systems is much higher (25–30%).

In a survey on the Isle of Wight, metering reduced consumption by 21%. In the National Metering Trial of 1989–93 in twelve locations, mostly in southern and central England, metering was found to reduce consumption by an average of 11%.

Leakage detection and elimination is seen as an effective means of increasing the available water supply. One quarter of all leakages occur within the household system, which is the responsibility of the householder, not the water company.

1.5   Minimisation of water usage

Water is increasingly seen as a scarce commodity, even in the temperate zones of the world. By 1992 eastern England was into its fourth year of drought with rivers that provided half the region's water needs flowing at well below average. A number of measures can be taken to reduce water consumption across the spectrum of society.

The heaviest use of water in households is in flushing human wastes into the sewerage system. In the traditional flush system some 9–13.5 litres of water are used at each flush. Systems are now available where the flush can be either 9 litres or 4.5 litres. One type of system only flushes as long as the handle is pressed and can therefore be stopped as soon as the pan is clear. There are also systems that use a vacuum (generated by an electrical pump) and a small amount of water (1 litre) to transport waste from the toilet to the treatment plant. There are now systems that do not use water at all – these are discussed in Section 5.9.14. Domestic appliances such as washing machines and dishwashers are also being designed with low water consumption rates.

Industry, faced with rising water costs, is minimising water usage in process operations wherever possible. Savings in water usage also translate into lower costs for treatment of the lower volume of effluent generated. In many plants the effluent is treated on-site and reused. On the domestic scene, many householders irrigate gardens with bath and kitchen waste waters.

Agriculture, though not a major user of water, can also play its part in water conservation. For instance, drip-feed irrigation systems (Figure 2) can be used in place of spray irrigation units. Drip-feed systems ensure efficient use of water by conveying it directly, either on the land surface or the subsurface, to the root zone of the crops where it is needed most. To reduce loss by evaporation, irrigation should be carried out at night or early in the morning when the air temperature is low.

Figure 2   *A section of a drip-feed irrigation system.*

Not all uses of water require a high-quality potable-grade supply. For instance, cooling processes in industry often use river water which has been given minimal treatment (e.g. screening to remove gross solids and chlorination to inhibit microbiological growth in pipelines). A further example is on ships and offshore oil and gas platforms where sea water is used for toilet flushing. In such instances two water distribution networks are required – one carrying potable water for drinking, washing, bathing and cooking purposes, and the other carrying lower quality water for non-potable uses.

Such networks have to be well designed to prevent cross-contamination of the potable supply by the non-potable line. Using such dual distribution systems, potable water can be conserved. In Kuwait City, a dual distribution system takes potable water and **brackish water** to homes, where the latter is used for watering plants in gardens. In the UK rain water collected from roof run-off can be used for watering plants, thus saving potable supplies.

1.6   Alleviation of water shortage in the south and south-east of England

The south and south-east of England are the driest parts of the UK and could suffer from serious water shortage in the future when the population increases. Several plans for alleviation of the anticipated water shortage have been put forward. In the late 1960s the installation of a desalination plant at Ipswich was considered but ruled out on grounds of cost. In recent years much effort has been devoted to detecting and remedying leakage in distribution networks. Anglian Water plans to install water meters to restrict rising water demand among its domestic customers, and more reservoirs are to be built to trap rain water which would otherwise run off into the sea. These reservoirs could also be used in water transfer schemes whereby water from the wetter north and west could be transferred by canals and pipelines to the drier south and south-east. Water transfer schemes have been used before. The first such scheme was said to have been initiated in the sixteenth century with the New River (an artificial river) bringing water from Hertfordshire to London. The Victorians brought water from the Lake District to Manchester, and from Wales to Birmingham. Indirect effluent reuse is another means of augmenting available water. This already happens in the Thames region – treated effluent is discharged into the River Thames and is subsequently re-abstracted for water supply. In the future, treated effluent could be discharged to underground aquifers and then re-abstracted for use.

1.7   Summary

The main consumers of water are the public, the electricity generating companies, industry and agriculture. Metering and billing of water supplies tends to reduce water usage and wastage. Measures to minimise water usage are possible in the domestic, industrial and agricultural sectors. Low water consumption toilet units and domestic appliances, drip-feed irrigation and dual distribution systems are possible options to adopt. Leakage elimination can significantly increase the available water supply. Water reuse and the use of rain water can also conserve potable supplies. Water transfer and indirect effluent reuse may see greater usage in the future in the south and south-east of England.

SAQ 2

List the ways in which potable water usage and leakage may be minimised.

See answer
for notes

2   THE HYDROLOGICAL CYCLE

2.1   Introduction

Having examined the demand for water in the UK, we shall now look at water resources and how they are formed through the **hydrological cycle** (first introduced in Unit 2).

The continuous cycling of water between land, open water surfaces and the sea, either directly or indirectly, is an extremely complex process. The identifiable mechanisms of the cycle are complicated not only by the characteristics of air–water–land interfaces across which the cycle operates, but also by climatic factors which vary in both time and space. The various operations and mechanisms within the cycle are illustrated in Figure 3 and are described below.

2.2   Evaporation

At an interface with the atmosphere, water changes its state from a liquid to a vapour in response to an increase in temperature caused by an external heat source. This temperature change is normally the result of either direct or indirect solar radiation. The transfer of moisture into the air is called evaporation. The process is also controlled by the relative humidity, or level of vapour saturation, of the air. The greater the relative humidity of the air, the less likely it is that evaporation will take place for a given temperature. In addition to the direct controls of temperature and humidity the rate of evaporation is also influenced by wind velocity, since continuous wind currents will carry away saturated air from the water surface, allowing more water to evaporate from the surface.

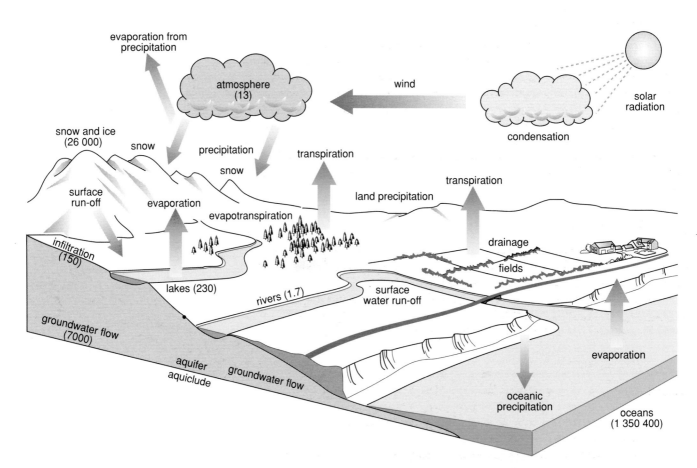

Figure 3   *The hydrological cycle (volumes are in Tm³ = 10¹² m³).*

Evaporation is variable with both time and place because the controlling factors themselves provide transient conditions. It will occur almost continuously from stretches of permanent open water and intermittently, but usually at a lower rate, from land surfaces.

Over land surfaces the rate of evaporation varies with the extent to which the ground is saturated. If the soil saturation level (i.e. the level to which all the voids are filled with water) is shallow, water moves up to the surface by the effect of capillary action. This controls the rate at which water will evaporate. Evaporation takes place from a sandy soil saturated up to the surface as quickly as it will from a lake, but the evaporation rate from saturated loam and clay soils is only 75–90% of that from an open body of water.

As it begins to rain, a large proportion of the water droplets is intercepted by the leaves of trees and other vegetation before reaching the ground. By this process of interception, water held on leaves and branches is returned rapidly to the atmosphere by evaporation. In forested areas, as much as 40% of light rain may be intercepted by foliage, although overall, the fraction is probably nearer to 10–25%.

2.3   Transpiration

If there was no vegetation, the rate of evaporation from land surfaces after rain would diminish rapidly to a very low value. Plants increase this rate by transpiration. In this process water is transferred from the soil through the roots to the leaves by osmosis and capillary action. Water evaporates from the surface of the leaves and the resulting vapour diffuses into the atmosphere. For hydrological measurements, this phenomenon is frequently lumped with evaporation because the two processes are not truly distinguishable using simple observational techniques over an area of mixed land use. The complete process of removal of moisture to the atmosphere from land surfaces by evaporation and transpiration is then termed evapotranspiration.

2.4   Condensation

As air rises it expands, owing to the decrease in pressure with height, and as it expands it cools at an average rate of 1°C for every 100 m of altitude. As the air cools, it becomes saturated with water vapour which condenses around small particles in the air. These particles may occur naturally, such as soil particles or salt particles residual to evaporation of sea spray, or they may be produced artificially during combustion. A measure of the necessary cooling to produce condensation is the dewpoint, which is the temperature at which air of a given absolute humidity and at a given pressure begins to give up its water as drops of dew. When moist air is chilled to a temperature below its dewpoint, in the presence of suitable minute particles, cloud or mist will form.

2.5   Air circulation

At this stage air circulation enters and plays a dual role. Firstly, winds or advective currents transmit moisture horizontally from one location to another. In this way moisture derived from oceanic evaporation can be transported many miles to a land mass. Secondly, convective or vertical currents arising from unequal heating or cooling can transmit moisture upwards. When it cools, some of the water vapour condenses. It is from these currents that most precipitation develops.

2.6   Precipitation

Precipitation may be in the form of rain, snow or hail, or in minor forms such as dew and hoar frost, but existing theories do not yet satisfactorily account for all the observed characteristics. In tropical climates precipitation occurs as a result of the gradual coalescence of the tiny condensed droplets as they collide within the cloud layer. In cooler climates, the formation of ice crystals in the upper levels of the cloud in turn is followed by crystal growth at the expense of water droplets and this results in snow or hail. When sufficient growth has been made, the large water drops or ice crystals have a larger ratio of mass to surface area than the small water drops or ice crystals.

The increased mass to surface area ratio allows the large drops to fall more rapidly than the small drops and they separate from the cloud. The small drops with very low velocity remain in the air currents associated with the cloud.

The large-scale cooling needed to give significant amounts of precipitation is achieved by lifting the air. There are three lifting processes and these are used to describe the type of precipitation. They are:

1   frontal (or cyclonic) – resulting from warm moist air meeting cooler air;

2   orographic – upward deflection of warm air streams by mountains;

3   convective – uplift associated with local heating by solar radiation.

In the hydrological cycle the total volume of water remains constant. The volume of water precipitated must necessarily balance the volume evaporated (when considered over a sufficiently long period of time to make variation in atmospheric storage of moisture insignificant).

2.7   Infiltration

Entry of precipitation through the soil surface into the soil and on downwards, by gravity, is known as infiltration. The rate at which this process can take place is governed by permeability (a measure of the ease with which water can flow through the subsurface layer) and by the existing degree of saturation of the soil. Infiltration can be impeded by outcropping impermeable rocks or by paved areas and also by the presence of fine-grained soils with a low permeability. At certain times it will be inhibited by frozen ground or saturated soil, and in Arctic areas by frozen subsoil the whole year round.

The total amount of infiltration will depend upon the rate at which it can take place, and upon the time available for water to seep into the ground. Clearly, rapid run-off of water will reduce the time available for infiltration and decrease the total amount taken into the ground.

2.8   Surface run-off

In some inland drainage areas all water is removed by evaporation and infiltration. However, precipitation not penetrating the land surface usually runs off the surface along defined channels which have been produced by geological processes, previous storms, or possibly by people to accelerate the process. Its eventual destination is the ocean, except, of course, where it runs to inland seas such as the Dead Sea. It is in the run-off phase of the cycle that physical intervention by humans has been greatest. People have:

(a)   harnessed the potential energy of rivers to provide power;

(b)   curbed erosion in order to protect dwellings and avoid the loss of fertile soil;

(c)   impounded water for supply schemes;

(d)   diverted flow for the irrigation of crops and to facilitate navigation; and

(e)   drained land to improve its agricultural value.

2.9   Percolation

Movement of infiltrated water downwards through the zone of aeration (Figure 4) is known as percolation. The infiltrated water which does not remain held by capillary forces in the surface soils moves by the action of gravity through the unsaturated layers of soil or rock until it arrives at the water table. Here the percolated water joins the body of ground water which seeps slowly to the sea.

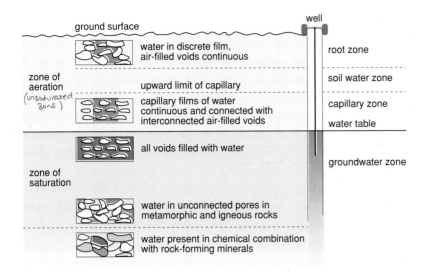

Figure 4   *Zones of subsurface water.*

2.10   *Aquifers*

Ground water is water that, after infiltrating and percolating through surface soils, flows in an *aquifer*, an underground water-bearing layer of porous rock. About one-third of the UK's drinking water is drawn from aquifers.

To permit economic development, an aquifer must be able to transmit large quantities of water from one point to another and therefore it must have a high permeability. The ground water contained in aquifers is released from springs and and can be responsible for the bulk of river flows.

Usually, aquifers are alluvial sands and gravels, the coarser sedimentary rocks such as sandstone, and rocks such as limestone in which chemical action has increased the water-bearing capacity. The strata of relatively impermeable rocks that lie either above or below confined aquifers (aquifers trapped between two impervious layers of rock) are called aquicludes.

The flow of ground water takes place through the layer that is completely saturated. This layer, not surprisingly, is called the zone of saturation (see Figure 4).

2.11   *Storage*

In a given fixed space at any phase of the hydrological cycle, there is an inflow and an outflow of water, the rates of which vary with time. The total cumulative difference between inflow and outflow is called storage. So within that space there is a body of water whose mass is not directly controlled by instantaneous values of inflow and outflow. For example, in river flow the movement of the whole body of water in the channel is generally downstream, yet a given reach contains a volume whose size may not change very much over a period of settled, fairly dry weather. Also, water may be abstracted from this body at a greater rate than the current inflow.

The storage element is most stable when it is large in relation to input and output quantities. This implies that the stored volume of water is stable in large lakes and reservoirs and also in aquifers, where the inflow and outflow rates are naturally low. As the size of the system increases, so also does the stability.

In our discussion of the hydrological cycle we have presumed that the system is completely stable, so both inflow and outflow are zero. This assumes that water present in the hydrological cycle was formed at a very early stage in geological time. However, there is a theory that suggests that water is continuing to form in the earth's core. Water is formed in small quantities, of course, by a number of artificial processes (e.g. in car exhausts). We have also assumed that no water is lost to the system by escaping from the earth's gravitational pull.

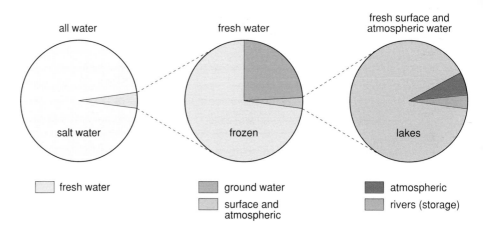

Figure 5   *Components of world water storage.*

The concept of storage is vital to the supply of water, since a major problem of supply revolves around the provision of water at the right time. Water is, naturally, in highest demand in dry weather and we seek constantly to exploit or increase the existing storage potential in the cycle.

The relative contributions to total storage are summarised in Figure 3, Figure 5 and Table 3. The oceans of the world hold the bulk of the water on earth.

Table 3   *Total available water in the various storage components of the hydrological cycle*

Storage component	Volume of water/(10^{12} m^3)	Volume/% (approx.)
Oceans	1 350 400	97.6
Ice caps and glaciers	26 000	1.9
Ground water and soil moisture	7150	0.5
Freshwater lakes	125	0.009
Saline lakes	105	0.008
Rivers	1.7	0.0001
Atmosphere	13	0.001

2.12   Summary

The hydrological cycle is a complex process involving evaporation, transpiration, condensation, air circulation, precipitation, infiltration, percolation and surface run-off. Aquifers are an important source of fresh water supplying about one-third of the UK's potable water demand. Most of the world's water is present as saline water in the oceans.

SAQ 3

What fraction of the total volume of water that circulates in the earth's hydrological cycle does river water represent? 12×10^{-6}

SAQ 4

What are the components of the hydrological cycle which can modify the volume of groundwater resources?   *See answer*

SAQ 5

Which of the following is the best description of evapotranspiration?

A   Transfer of water from the oceans, seas and land surface to the air.
B   The accelerated process of transfer of moisture to the air at a water–air interface caused by an external heat source.
C   Transfer of moisture from soil to the air through roots and leaves and plants.
D   Items B and C together.
E   The total removal of moisture to the atmosphere from land surfaces.

SAQ 6

How do the following affect infiltration?
(a) Dense vegetation.   reduce by incr evapotranspiration ← see answer
(b) Steeply sloping land surface.   reduce by incr. run-off
(c) Cultivated land.   increase
(d) Roads and buildings.   decrease by increasing run-off

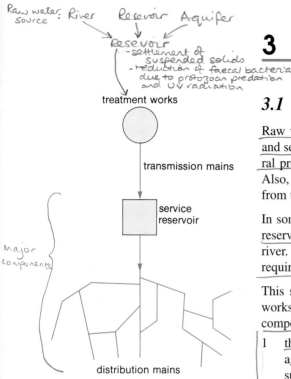

Figure 6 handwritten annotations:
Raw water source: River   Reservoir   Aquifer
Reservoir
  - settlement of suspended solids
  - reduction of faecal bacteria due to protozoan predation and UV radiation

treatment works

transmission mains

service reservoir

Major components

distribution mains

Figure 6   *A water distribution network.*

3   WATER SUPPLY

3.1   Introduction

Raw water is usually abstracted from a river and pumped to a reservoir for storage and settlement. In the reservoir, the number of faecal bacteria is reduced through natural processes such as predation by protozoa and **ultraviolet radiation** from sunlight. Also, a large portion of the suspended solids settles out. The water is then conveyed from the reservoir to a treatment works.

In some situations, particularly in hilly areas, rain water is abstracted from a storage reservoir made by damming a valley in an upland catchment area, instead of from a river. In other instances, water may be drawn from aquifers. (These waters usually require little treatment due to their unpolluted nature – see Section 4.12.)

This section is concerned with the plant used in carrying water from the treatment works to the houses, farms, blocks of flats and buildings of the community. The major components of the distribution network are shown in Figure 6 and comprise:

1   the service reservoir, which must balance the fluctuating demands of the users against the steady output from the source of supply as well as provide a backup supply should there be a breakdown at the source;

2   the pipelines or 'mains' with their associated valves and fittings, which must carry the required quantities of water between the different parts of the system.

3.2   Service reservoirs

Transmission mains convey treated water from the water treatment works to the service reservoir throughout all, or most of, the day. However, as with the demand for electricity or gas, the demand for water varies with the time of day. Typically, the water demand at night is about 20% less than the average daily demand, whereas the peak demand, occurring around midday, is about 40% greater than the average daily demand.

Figure 7(a) shows the cumulative volume of water entering and leaving a service reservoir during the day. The straight line of constant slope represents the constant rate of inflow (supply) to the reservoir, and the variable line running at first below and then above the supply line represents the changing demand from the reservoir. Figure 7(a) is an example of a mass diagram for a reservoir. The effect of variations between supply and demand on the level of water in the reservoir is shown in Figure 7(b).

For example, starting at midnight, the water level in the reservoir is H. During the early hours of the morning, supply exceeds demand and the water level in the

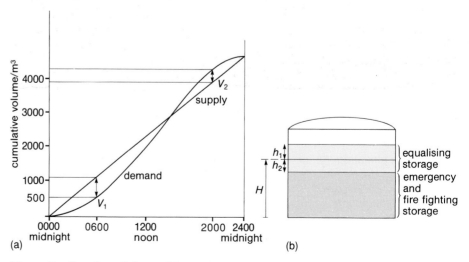

Figure 7   *Supply and demand in service reservoirs: (a) mass diagram; (b) reservoir levels.*

reservoir increases. By 0600 hours the level has reached a maximum value $H + h_1$. This corresponds to the situation shown on the mass diagram where 1100 m³ has been supplied to the reservoir, whereas only 500 m³ has been withdrawn. This represents a surplus V_1 of 600 m³.

After 0600 hours the rate of demand increases (as the nation awakes) and by 1500 hours the level in the reservoir has returned to its initial level H with supply matching demand exactly.

By early evening the situation has reversed. At 2000 hours, the mass diagram shows that the deficit V_2 between the amount of water supplied and that withdrawn is 400 m³, at which time the water in the reservoir has reached its lowest level, $H - h_2$.

Thereafter, water demand 'eases off' again with the water level in the reservoir rising back to its initial level at midnight.

The volume $V_1 + V_2$ is called the equalising storage, because it performs the function of equalising supply and demand. Without equalising storage the transmission mains would need to be large enough to cope with peak demand and would be underutilised most of the time. With a service reservoir the transmission mains need only carry the average daily demand (together with an extra 15–25% to account for leakage). Extra capacity may be incorporated in a service reservoir, in addition to equalising storage, for emergency and fire-fighting use. Such an extra capacity is shown in Figure 7(b).

Usually service reservoirs (Figure 8) are constructed of concrete and frequently, for reasons of both economy and appearance, they are sunk wholly or partly below ground level. The reservoir needs to be positioned with sufficient elevation to provide an adequate flow to the distribution area and to raise the water to the top of buildings. The elevation of the water surface in a reservoir above some datum is a measure of the static head of water available (Figure 9). For example, the elevation of the reservoir level above Point A in Figure 9 is 50 m. So the static head at A is 50 m. In other words, the water pressure available to the house at A is equivalent to the pressure at the base of a 50 m high column of water. At point B in Figure 9, near the top of the

Figure 8   *Prestressed concrete service reservoirs of capacities 11 362 m³.*

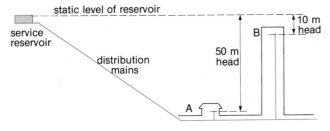

Figure 9   *Static head in distribution mains.*

high-rise building, the static head is only 10 m. The pipes taking water from the service reservoir to their points of usage are called distribution mains.

In a distribution main, the head should not be lower than 30 m for fire-fighting purposes and should not exceed 70 m to avoid wastage, wear and noise in the pipework. Many domestic fittings, including taps, ball valves, stopcocks and domestic washing machines are designed to operate at moderate pressure. At high pressures, wear of fittings becomes excessive, seals need frequent replacement and the system is noisy and more liable to 'knocking' and vibration caused by the sudden closing of a tap. The sudden closing of the tap stops a long, moving column of water and this creates a surge in the supply pipe. This surge is called water hammer. Furthermore, at high pressures the system is likely to leak at an increasing rate (see Section 1.4).

Pressure-reducing valves are sometimes used if the water pressure is too high. These valves are designed to limit the pressure downstream of the valve to a predetermined value, irrespective of the pressure upstream. Alternatively, in flat areas, where elevated sights for ground level tanks are not available, or where it is necessary to supply tall buildings, water towers (Figure 10) may be used. In exceptional cases, tall buildings may require their own system of pumps to raise water to the top.

Figure 11 shows a possible arrangement of service reservoirs, water towers, mains and buildings. We can see how the arrangement of the reservoir is used to create appropriate pressure zones.

Figure 10 *Water tower.*

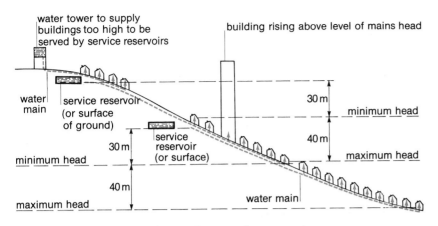

Figure 11 *Distribution of water from service reservoirs.*

It is not always possible to take advantage of flow under gravity in transmission or in drainage and sewerage systems. The necessary head for flow then has to be raised by pumping through part or all of the pipeline. Where pumping occurs, the pipeline is called a rising main.

In England and Wales, water companies are legally required to provide fire hydrants as requested by the fire service, but there is no guidance on the quantity of water to be made available or its pressure. Nevertheless, fire-fighting requirements govern the size of main that is considered to be desirable. When a pipe is fed from both ends (e.g. in a loop), a diameter of 75 mm is usually considered to be satisfactory. A 100-mm diameter pipe is preferred where only one end is fed. If the fire service considers that there would be insufficient water available for quenching a fire, it will ask for a larger main. Under these circumstances the extra cost is borne by the fire service, both for the larger main and for the provision and maintenance of the hydrant.

SAQ 7

Figure 12 shows the hourly variation of demand from a service reservoir. Plot a mass diagram for the service reservoir and estimate the volume of equalising storage required.

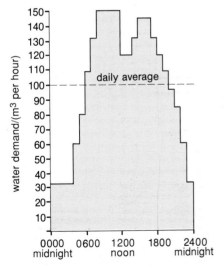

plot graph of cumulative volume m³ against time then ?

Figure 12 *Hourly variation in demand from service reservoir.*

SAQ 8

Match the components (A, B, C) of a distribution system with the circumstances in which they would be required as listed under options 1 to 4.

A   Storage tower *1,2,3*

B   Spur water main of diameter 100 mm
    1 poss 3

C   Pressure-reducing valve
    4

1   To meet fire-fighting requirements

2   To give a reasonable water pressure at the top of a tall building on flat land

3   To avoid a water head of less than 30 m

4   To avoid a water head of greater than 70 m

3.3   *Transmission mains*

The water from service reservoirs is distributed by a network of pipes of various sizes, laid beneath the streets, pavements and verges of our towns and cities. Any part of a distribution system can be isolated by valves at appropriate points. Figure 13 shows both a loop (as at A) and a spur or dead end (as at B) within a typical distribution lay-out. Looped or ring mains are always preferred to spurs or dead ends because when the rate of flow is restricted in a long spur, the water will remain there for a long time, and its quality may deteriorate. In the event of repair work, the whole length may need to be isolated. In a ring system, water can flow through a lightly loaded section to meet demands elsewhere. There is also the advantage that one section of a ring may be isolated without cutting off the sections on either side. For example, the section ab of the ring main shown in Figure 13 may be isolated. However, water could still flow in sections ac and cb. The distribution grid is arranged so that any pipe can be taken out of service without cutting off the output to the others.

A mains pipeline can be subject to a variety of loading conditions. There is the static loading due to the internal water pressure in the pipe. Also, pipelines are often subject to water hammer. Changes in flow direction and velocity at bends, contractions, expansions and partly closed valves lead to additional loading on the pipe, as does the thermal expansion or contraction of the pipe material.

The choice of pipe material clearly depends on the magnitude and nature of these stresses. However, other factors have to be considered:

1   the ground conditions, in so far as these affect the possibilities of ground movement and corrosion;

2   the corrosive nature of the water;

3   the size of pipe;

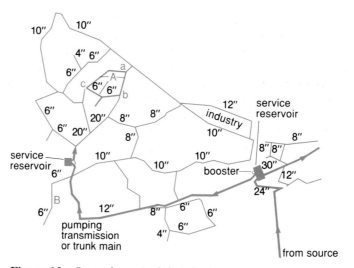

Figure 13   *Part of a typical distribution system.*

4   the ease of jointing;

5   the cost.

The joints between adjacent lengths of pipe must be watertight. Occasionally, joints are welded, but it is more usual to find some form of sealing ring contained in a socket at the end of one pipe or at each end of a separate collar.

Cost, as the last factor, is by no means the least important. It is usual to aim for the minimum overall cost. The materials used for transmission mains and their respective merits are listed in Table 4.

Table 4   *Materials used for transmission mains*

Material	Merits	Disadvantages
Steel	High strength and ductility resulting in light weight. Jointing easy with mechanical or (in large sizes) welded joints.	Requires careful protection against external and internal corrosion.
Cast iron	Modern ductile iron pipes have strength and ductility approaching those of steel. Push-fit joints are easy to make. The pipes are cast in an automatic machine to obtain light but strong walls free from imperfections.	Requires special protection against external corrosion in some types of ground. Often subject to growth of incrustations or tuberculations internally unless lined with concrete.
Asbestos cement	Economical and resistant to decay under most soil conditions. Light and easy to handle and lay.	Vulnerable to damage during handling.
UPVC (unplasticised polyvinyl chloride)	Light, easy to handle and install.	Deformation and stretching due to stress over a period of time.
Prestressed concrete	Sometimes economic in large sizes.	Heavy and somewhat inflexible in use. Cannot be cut on site and joints allow only limited angular deflection.

3.4   Summary

Raw water drawn for public supply from a river is usually stored in a reservoir before treatment. While in the reservoir, suspended solids settle out and faecal bacteria are reduced in number. The water from the reservoir is then sent to a treatment works. After treatment the water goes via transmission mains to service reservoirs which act to even out variations in consumption during a 24-hour demand period. Water is taken by distribution mains from the service reservoirs to the consumers. The head of water necessary for flow is provided by raising the service reservoir level or by pumping. A pumped pipeline is called a rising main. The size and construction material of mains pipelines depends on the quantity of water carried and the stresses imposed during use.

4   WATER TREATMENT

4.1   Introduction

Water for public supply can, as mentioned previously, be obtained from underground sources by wells sunk into aquifers or from surface sources such as purpose-built reservoirs or lakes and rivers. All these sources can be subject to pollution. In the case of underground water, polluted surface water can enter the saturation zone of an aquifer and so lead to its contamination. Pollution can come from waste tip *leachate* containing any *heavy metals* and organic compounds, farm run-off containing nitrates and *pesticides*, and industrial wastes which may have been deliberately dumped down old coal mine shafts. River water can be affected by farm drainage, sewage works and industrial effluents and also the run-off water from roads. Thus there is a need to maintain the quality of the aquatic environment to ensure that the water is suitable for treatment for public supply and that the cost of treatment is kept as low as possible.

TMA Q1

As explained in Units 5–6, the EC directives on water quality cover both underground and surface water and pay attention to the quality of water abstracted for drinking purposes and the quality of the treated water in the public supply. The 1989 Water Act has incorporated the EC Directive on the Quality of Drinking Water into its regulations.

In this section we shall be looking at the treatment of water after it has been abstracted from a suitable source. The 1989 Water Act has given a definition of wholesomeness as applied to water (see Units 5–6).

With this in mind the functions of water treatment can be considered as:

1   the removal of suspended matter and rendering of the water clean, colourless and free from disagreeable taste and odour;

2   the disinfection of the water so that the numbers of bacteria are reduced to the appropriate level;

3   the removal of chemicals harmful to health and the reduction to low levels of chemicals that might otherwise interfere with normal domestic and industrial requirements;

4   the reduction of the corrosive properties of the water and protection of the pipe supply system;

5   the minimisation of the amount of material passing into the supply system which might encourage biological growth.

The basic treatment for river water is shown in Figure 14. It should be noted that not all the processes shown will be required for every water. The treatment used will depend on the quality of the abstracted water. For a water that has little pollution it may only be necessary to use preliminary settlement, rapid sand filtration and chlorination, whereas a poor quality water may require even more treatment than shown.

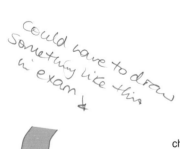
Could have to draw Something like this in exam

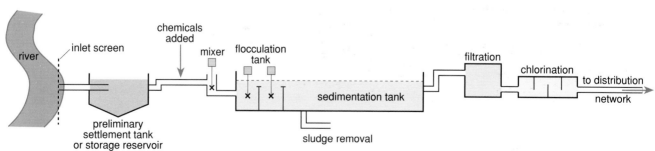

Figure 14   *Diagram of a typical water treatment process.*

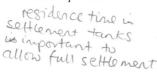
residence time in settlement tanks is important to allow full settlement

4.2 *Preliminary treatment*

The abstracted water is first screened to remove suspended and floating debris, such as leaves or branches, which could interfere with the operation of machinery in the treatment works. The water then enters a preliminary settlement tank or storage reservoir. It then passes through *screens* again and goes to the treatment works. Screens may be classified by the size of their openings as coarse or fine, and may be in the form of bars or continuous belts. Coarse screens are used primarily to protect the treatment works from physical damage, while the fine screens serve to remove material which might eventually block pipework in the system. Coarse screens usually consist of a series of metal bars spaced 5–15 cm apart. Fine screens, which follow the coarse screens, have a bar spacing of 10–25 mm. Screens are positioned in the inlet channel of the treatment plant at an angle of 60° to facilitate removal of the collected material or *screenings* by raking. The cleaning of the screens is important to prevent them choking. *Bar screens* can be raked by hand but are more usually cleaned by a mechanical raking operation, either on a time basis or by pressure-sensing probes which are activated by an excessive head loss across the screen. A continuous chain scraper can also be used to clean bar screens (Figure 15).

A variation of the fine screen is the microstrainer (Figure 16). This consists of a rotating drum with a stainless steel micromesh fabric. The mesh size can range from 15–64 μm so that very fine suspended matter such as algae and plankton can be trapped. The trapped solids are dislodged from the fabric by high-pressure water jets using good quality water, and carried away for disposal.

Storage of the screened water in the preliminary settlement tank or reservoir smoothes out fluctuations in the water quality and helps to reduce the suspended solids content.

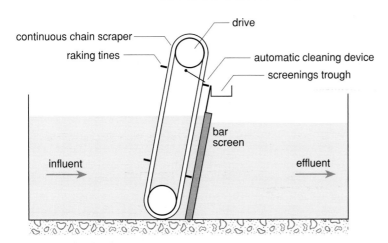

Figure 15   *The cleaning mechanism for a bar screen.*

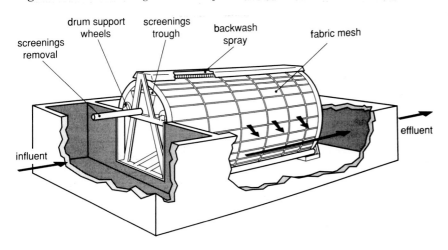

Figure 16   *A typical microstrainer.*

It also reduces the number of pathogenic bacteria present, and the oxidation which can occur will allow the degradation of organic matter and the precipitation of soluble iron and manganese as oxides and hydroxides. It is recommended that storage should be for at least seven days. The storage of water is particularly valuable when abstraction is not possible, e.g. during droughts, or when the water source is badly contaminated or in flood condition.

After preliminary settlement it may be necessary in the case of poor quality water with a low dissolved oxygen content to aerate the water. There are a number of ways in which this can be done but the simplest is to allow the water to fall over a series of steps so that it is able to entrain oxygen from the air. This is known as cascade aeration. In addition to increasing the oxygen content, aeration also helps to liberate soluble gases, such as carbon dioxide and hydrogen sulphide, and volatile organic compounds which could give an undesirable taste to the water.

Aeration can reduce the corrosiveness of raw waters which are acidic due to their carbonic acid content. When the water is aerated some of the dissolved carbon dioxide is displaced by the oxygen dissolving in the water. This causes some of the carbonic acid that has been formed in the water by the carbon dioxide to be converted back to carbon dioxide and water in order to maintain chemical equilibrium. (Refer to Unit 3 if you are unsure of any of the terms in this paragraph.)

As indicated in Units 5–6, aeration is also used to remove iron and manganese from solution. Iron and manganese can cause peculiar tastes and can stain clothing. Iron is soluble in water only in the absence of dissolved oxygen and at pH values below 6.5. Aeration converts soluble iron into its insoluble hydroxide which can then be removed by filtration. Manganese can be removed by the same principle.

After aeration, the water is passed through a fine screen before entering the treatment works proper.

4.3   Coagulation and flocculation

Coagulation is always considered along with *flocculation* and is used to remove particles which cannot be removed by sedimentation or filtration alone. These particles are usually less than 1 μm in size and are termed colloids. They have poor settling characteristics and are responsible for the colour and turbidity of water. They include clays, metal oxides, proteins, microorganisms and organic substances such as those that give the brown coloration to water from 'peaty' catchment areas. The important property which they all have is that they carry a negative charge and this, along with the interaction between the colloidal particles and the water, prevents them from aggregating and settling in still water. The particles can be aggregated by adding multivalent ions or colloids having an opposite (positive) charge. These are added as chemical coagulants.

Chemicals commonly used as coagulants in water treatment are aluminium and ferric salts which will be present as the ions Al^{3+} and Fe^{3+}. (Recall from Unit 4 that 20 tonnes of aluminium sulphate was accidentally tipped into the public water supply at **Camelford** on 6 July 1988.) These positively charged ions neutralise the naturally occurring negatively charged particles, thus allowing the particles to aggregate. At high concentrations of aluminium or ferric salts, and in the presence of sufficient alkalinity, insoluble hydroxides of aluminium or iron are formed (see below). In the precipitation reaction the colloidal particles are enmeshed within the precipitate and thus removed.

$$Al_2(SO_4)_3 + 3Ca(HCO_3)_2 \rightleftharpoons 2Al(OH)_3 + 3CaSO_4 + 6CO_2$$

aluminium	calcium	aluminium	calcium	carbon
sulphate	bicarbonate	hydroxide	sulphate	dioxide

If there is inadequate alkalinity in the water, it can be added in the form of lime (calcium hydroxide) or soda ash (sodium carbonate).

In some waters, even with the optimum dose of coagulant, coagulation is poor and so it is necessary to add extra substances known as coagulant aids. These aids can be clay, silica or **polyelectrolytes**. Polyelectrolytes are long-chain organic molecules with chemical groups attached along the length of the chain, which becomes charged when the molecule is dissolved in water. The negative colloidal particles are attracted to positively charged chemical groups on the polyelectrolyte. Polyelectrolytes can be used either on their own or in conjunction with inorganic coagulants.

After the coagulants are added, the water is mixed rapidly in a mixing chamber using a high-speed turbine. Once coagulation has taken place, a very fine precipitate or floc will form. To aid this floc to coalesce with neighbouring particles and grow into larger flocs with more settleable masses, the water is gently stirred. The process of coalescence is known as flocculation. The gentle stirring can be achieved using paddles to induce a rolling motion in the water, and this continues for some 20–45 minutes. After this treatment the water is passed for sedimentation.

4.4 Sedimentation

When water has little or no movement, suspended solids sink to the bottom under the force of gravity and form a sediment. This process is called **sedimentation**. In water treatment it is used to remove solids from waters which are high in sediment content, and also to remove particles rendered settleable by coagulation and flocculation.

The theory of sedimentation would seem to be quite simple. Make the settling tank large enough and the flow slow enough and then calculate the rate of fall of the sediment.

What other factors do you think need to be known?

It will be necessary to know the density and the size of the particles to calculate their rate of fall. There should be no turbulence in the tank as it will tend to reduce settlement and there must be an even flow through the tank to prevent a narrow stream flowing through quickly from one end to the other (channelling).

Because of these factors we shall now look at settlement in greater detail. Sedimentation tanks can be of various types: rectangular with horizontal flow, circular with **radial flow**, or hopper-bottomed with upward flow (Figure 17).

The circular and rectangular tanks are equipped with mechanical sludge-scraping devices to remove the wet sludge that has settled. In hopper-bottomed tanks the sludge concentrates at the bottom of the hopper from where it can be drawn off. In radial and horizontal flow tanks any floating material is skimmed from the surface by a blade carried by the scraping mechanism, and is discharged to be combined with the settled sludge. In upward flow tanks this material is removed manually.

An idealised representation of a circular radial flow tank is shown in Figure 18. There are four important zones in the tank:

(a) Inlet zone – at the central well, which has a round baffle plate, the flow is established in a uniform radial direction so that short-circuiting does not take place.

(b) Settling zone – where settling is assumed to occur as the water flows towards the outlet.

(c) Outlet zone – in which the flow converges up and over the decanting weirs.

(d) Sludge zone – where settled material collects and is pumped out.

The performance of a settling tank is related to the settling velocity of the fine particles in suspension. The settling velocity is the speed at which the particles move downwards under gravity through the suspension. The retention time required by the particles to settle to the bottom of a settling tank is related to the settling velocity by the simple relationship:

$$\text{retention time} = \frac{\text{depth of settling zone}}{\text{settling velocity}} \tag{1}$$

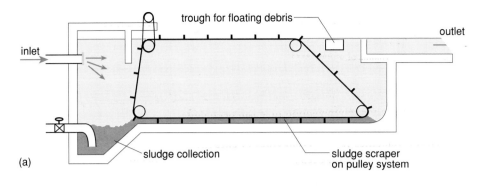

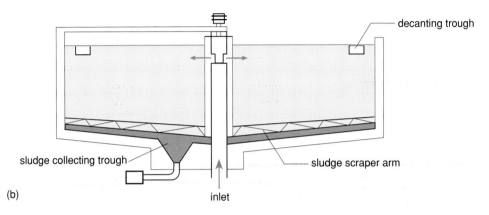

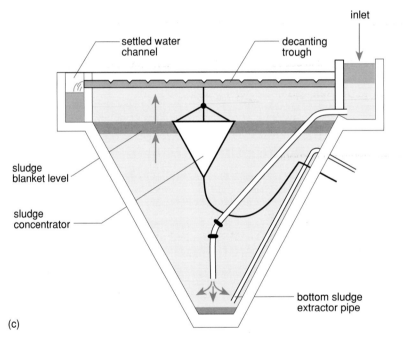

Figure 17   *Typical sedimentation tanks: (a) rectangular horizontal flow tank; (b) circular radial flow tank; (c) upflow tank.* or hopper-bottomed sludge-blanket clarifier

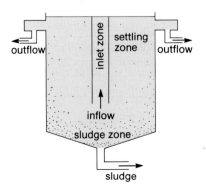

Figure 18   *Radial flow settling tank.*

The time available for particles to settle out in the settling tank also depends on the flow rate of the suspension through the tank:

$$\text{retention time} = \frac{\text{volume of settling zone}}{\text{flow rate through tank}} \qquad (2)$$

Table 5 shows settling velocities for various types of suspended solids and the required retention times for sedimentation in a 3-m deep tank.

Table 5 *Settling velocities for different types of suspended solids and the retention time required in a 3-m deep tank for sedimentation to occur*

Nature of solids	Settling velocity/ (mm s⁻¹)	Retention time for settling to occur in 3-m deep tank/h
Clay, silt	0.07	11.9
Primary organic waste	0.42	1.98
Aluminium and iron flocs	0.83	1.00
Activated sludge	2.00	0.42
Grit	20.00	0.042

It is clear that to achieve a separation of materials with low settling velocities, the retention time in the settling tank must be increased. In practice, this can be achieved by increasing the settling tank volume or decreasing the flow rate of suspension through the tank.

Exercise

100 m³ d⁻¹ of a suspension of silt is passed through a settling tank with a 3-m deep settling zone. What is the effective settling zone area?

Answer

From Table 5,

Retention time for 3-m depth = 11.9 hours

$$= \frac{11.9}{24} \text{ day}$$

Volume of settling zone = settling area × depth

$$= \text{flow rate} \times \text{retention time (from Equation 2)}$$

So, settling area $= \dfrac{\text{flow rate} \times \text{retention time}}{\text{depth}}$

$$= \frac{(100) \times (11.9/24)}{3} \text{ m}^2$$

$$= 16.5 \text{ m}^2$$

SAQ 9

A circular radial-flow tank has a settling zone depth of 4 m and a settling zone area of 700 m². What is the retention time necessary to remove organic detritus with settling velocities of 0.4 mm s⁻¹ and greater? What flow rate is required through the tank?

In order to achieve the required retention time in SAQ 9 the throughput of suspension must not be greater than 0.28 m³ s⁻¹. But what if the same suspension was passed through a 2-m deep tank – half the depth? One might expect that in a shallow tank the same particles would reach the sludge zone at the bottom more quickly. Would this allow a larger throughput? Halving the tank depth would halve the retention time of particles in the tank; but would also halve the tank volume. So the flow rate through the shallower tank would be the same as for the deep tank. This independence of settling behaviour with depth has led to the development of shallow depth sedimentation tanks in which the flow is passed in parallel through a number of closely spaced inclined channels arranged in a device called a parallel plate separator (Figure 19). The slope of the settling channels is steep so that the tank is continuously self-cleaning (the solids slide off and go to the bottom of the tank). The advantage of such an arrangement is clear. For the same tank area, with *n* channels, throughput can be increased *n*-fold whilst retaining the same settling velocity in each channel.

The discussion so far has dealt with 'ideal' conditions in which particles settle under gravity without hindrance from other particles in the vicinity. An example of such a situation would be the settling of heavy grit particles. There are, however, types of particles called flocculent particles which interact with other particles in their vicinity. An example would be organic suspended solids with a broad spectrum of sizes and surface characteristics.

Different-sized particles settle at different rates so that larger particles will overtake or collide with smaller particles. These collisions may result in coalescence into larger aggregates with an increasing settling velocity so that the typical path of a flocculent particle is curved (Figure 20) indicating the increasing velocity with depth. One important requirement of settling tanks for treating flocculent suspensions is therefore that the depth should be great enough to provide the opportunity for particle agglomeration to occur. This is in contrast to the behaviour of discrete particles whose settling behaviour is independent of depth. The effect of tank depth on removal efficiency is shown in Figure 20. If the tank depth is reduced by half, the retention time is halved and the depth reached by each type of particle during that time is reduced. Nevertheless the discrete particle will again just reach the bottom of the reduced depth tank, whereas the flocculent particle will not have reached the tank floor and will be drawn off in the tank outflow. This is a simplification of what actually happens inside a sedimentation tank; however, it is generally considered that the overall effect of reducing settling tank depth is to reduce removal efficiency when treating flocculent particles.

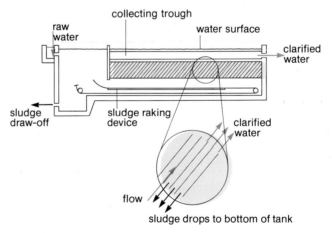

Figure 19   *A parallel plate separator within a sedimentation tank.*

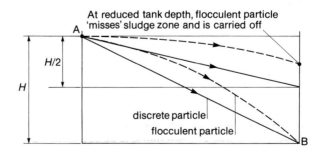

Figure 20   *Effect of tank depth on removal of discrete and flocculent particles.*

Settlement tanks must therefore be designed deep enough to allow all particles to settle, and also to have flow such that settled solids are not disturbed and carried over the weir at the outlet of the settlement tank.

An important parameter therefore in settlement tanks is the rate at which water flows over the weir, known as weir overflow rate, expressed as:

$$\frac{\text{maximum flow per day}}{\text{total length of weir}} = m^3 \ m^{-1} \ d^{-1}$$

Typical values for the weir overflow rate range from 300 to 450 $m^3 \ m^{-1} \ d^{-1}$.

Exercise

A rectangular horizontal flow sedimentation tank has floor dimensions 10 m × 30 m. The maximum flow through the tank is 8000 m^3 per day. What is the weir overflow rate, the weir being on the shorter side of the tank?

Answer

The weir overflow rate $= \dfrac{\text{maximum flow per day}}{\text{total length of weir}}$

$$= \frac{8000 \ m^3 \ d^{-1}}{10 \ m}$$

$$= 800 \ m^3 \ m^{-1} \ d^{-1}$$

This overflow rate exceeds the accepted criterion of 300–450 $m^3 \ m^{-1} \ d^{-1}$ and if used would tend to disturb the settled sludge. An acceptable value can be obtained by increasing the effective weir length. This can be achieved by increasing the breadth of the tank, but this would take up more land and be costly. An alternative and less costly solution would be to insert V-notches in the weir and so effectively increase the weir length, or have a suspended collection trough at the end of the tank so that the effluent could flow into the trough from either side, thus doubling the weir length. In our example the effective weir length could be doubled by using a trough and the overflow rate would be reduced to a more acceptable 400 $m^3 \ m^{-1} \ d^{-1}$.

Another parameter to be noted is the surface loading rate, which is expressed as

$$\frac{\text{maximum flow per day}}{\text{tank surface area}} = m^3 \ m^{-2} \ d^{-1}$$

Typical values for the surface loading rate range from 30 to 45 $m^3 \ m^{-2} \ d^{-1}$.

Exercise

What would the surface loading rate be for the rectangular sedimentation tank in the last exercise?

Answer

Surface loading rate $= \dfrac{\text{maximum flow per day}}{\text{tank surface area}}$

$$= \frac{8000 \ m^3 \ d^{-1}}{10 \times 30 \ m^2}$$

$$= 26.7 \ m^3 \ m^{-2} \ d^{-1}$$

SAQ 10

What length of effective weir would be required for a rectangular sedimentation tank with a maximum flow of 0.25 m^3 per second if the weir overflow rate is to be 350 $m^3 \ m^{-1} \ d^{-1}$?

In the UK, upward-flow or hopper-bottomed sludge-blanket clarifiers (Figure 17c) are extremely popular. This type of tank is an inverted cone with the flocculated water entering from the bottom of the cone. Because the cross-sectional area of the tank increases rapidly from the apex (at the bottom) to the base of the cone (at the top) the upward velocity of the water is reduced as it rises. In the tank there will therefore be a horizontal plane where the upward water velocity equals the average downward rate of fall of the floc. This results in the formation of a horizontal 'blanket' of floc suspended in the water. This blanket of floc acts as a filter through which the upward flowing water must pass. Maximum use of the tank is made when the top of the floc blanket is as high as possible in the tank. When the blanket becomes too dense it is removed by bleeding off the excess floc.

SAQ 11

Which of the following characteristics of raw water are greatly improved by coagulation, flocculation and sedimentation?

A   Colour. ✓
B   Taste. possibly
C   Clarity. ✓
D   Chloride concentration.
E   Nitrate concentration.

4.5   Flotation

An alternative technique to that of sedimentation is flotation. This uses gas bubbles to increase the buoyancy of suspended solids. The gas bubbles attach to the particles and make their effective density lower than that of the water. This causes the particles to rise through the water to float to the top. Flotation may be achieved by several methods but the most effective form is dissolved air flotation. In this process (Figure 21) air is dissolved in water at elevated pressures and then released as tiny bubbles (30–120 μm) by reducing the pressure to atmospheric level.

The principal advantages of flotation over sedimentation are that very small or light particles that settle slowly can be removed more completely and in a shorter time. Once the particles have reached the surface, they can be collected by a skimmer.(In Figure 21, the skimmer blades should touch the water surface.)

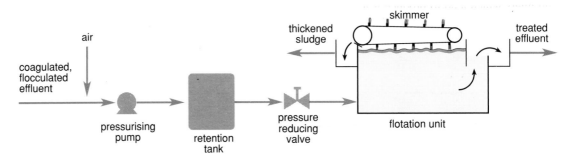

Figure 21   *Diagram of a dissolved air flotation system.*

4.6   *Filtration*

In filtration the partially treated water is passed through a medium such as sand or anthracite which acts as a 'strainer', retaining the fine organic and inorganic material and allowing clean water through. The action of filters is complex and in some types of filter biological action also takes place. Sand filters are used in water treatment to remove the fine particles which cannot be economically removed by sedimentation.

Mechanical straining of the water is only a minor part of the filtration process as the main process by which particles are retained is adsorption. In adsorption the particles adhere to the filter material or previously adsorbed particles. If a particle passes close to a solid surface, there may be either electrical attraction or repulsion, depending on the surface charges of both the particle and the solid surface.

Filtration in water treatment can be carried out using simple slow sand filters or, as is more usual for flocculated water, rapid gravity sand filters.

A slow sand filter consists of a shallow basin in which about a metre of sand rests on a gravel base, underneath which there is a system of collection pipes and channels for the filtered water. The water to be treated flows down through the filter bed and as it does so a layer a few millimetres thick of algae, plankton and other microscopic plant life forms on the top. This layer is known as the *Schmutzdecke*, which is German for film or deck of dirt. On this layer fine filtration takes place. In order to preserve this layer, the temperature and velocity of the inflow must be carefully controlled. Some biodegradation also takes place on the *Schmutzdecke* resulting in a reduction of the organic matter, nitrate and phosphate which may be present in the water.

When the rate of filtration begins to tail off, the filter is drained and the top 2 cm of sand removed to be replaced by fresh sand. Slow sand filters are expensive to build and operate, and require a large amount of space.

As their name suggests, slow sand filters do not supply the water at a fast enough rate, so they have been largely replaced by rapid gravity sand filters, which are particularly effective for water treated with coagulants and are less expensive than slow sand filters. Figure 22 shows a rapid gravity filter. The flow is some 20 times greater than in slow sand filters; hence a smaller filter (and therefore space) will be adequate. Because of the high rate of flow, no *Schmutzdecke* is formed and hence little or no biodegradation takes place in these filters. The filter is cleaned by pumping water (and sometimes air to assist in scouring) under pressure backwards through the filter to wash out the trapped impurities. This process is called ***backwashing***. Unlike slow sand filters which tend to produce water with a particularly low bacterial count, rapid filters give bacterial counts which are much higher, increasing the necessity to follow them with disinfection before supplying the water to the public.

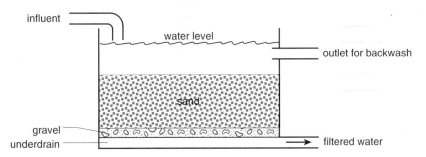

Figure 22   *Section through a rapid gravity sand filter.*

In many treatment plants where slow sand filtration is the key processing stage, rapid filtration is employed prior to the slow sand filter in a process called double sand filtration. In this arrangement the rapid gravity filters reduce the load of solid matter in the water before it goes to the slow sand filters. This allows a greater overall rate of treatment and the slow sand filters do not then need to be cleaned so often.

A variation of the filtering process is the use of a layer of large anthracite grains (1.2–2.5 mm) on top of a layer of smaller (0.5–1.0 mm) sand grains, which are denser and have a smaller 'intergrain' pore size. Anthracite–sand filters tend to clog less rapidly because some of the floc adheres to the larger anthracite grains before the water filters through the sand. This means that increased filtration rates are possible.

See answer for notes

SAQ 12

List the advantages and disadvantages of slow sand filters and rapid gravity filters.

4.7   Disinfection

Before treated water can be passed into the public supply, it is necessary to remove all potentially pathogenic microorganisms. Since these microorganisms are extremely small, it is not possible to guarantee their complete removal by sedimentation and filtration, so the water must be disinfected to ensure its quality. Disinfection is the inactivation of pathogenic organisms and is not to be confused with sterilisation which is the destruction of all organisms.

Chlorine is the most popular disinfecting agent for drinking water, although the use of ozone has recently become more widespread. Chlorine acts as a strong oxidising agent which can penetrate microbial cells, killing the microorganisms. It kills most bacteria but not all viruses. It is relatively cheap and extremely soluble in water (up to 7000 mg l^{-1}). It has some disadvantages. It can lead to the formation of trihalomethanes such as chloroform if organics are present in the water being disinfected. Trihalomethanes are considered to be carcinogenic and therefore undesirable. If, however, the water has been previously treated by coagulation and flocculation, the chances of organics being present to form trihalomethanes are remote. Chlorine is a dangerous chemical and so requires careful handling. It can also give rise to taste and odour problems: for example, in the presence of phenols it forms ***chlorophenols*** which have a strong medicinal odour and taste (see Unit 3).

When chlorine is dissolved in water the reaction is

$$Cl_2 + H_2O \rightleftharpoons HCl + HOCl$$

HOCl, hypochlorous acid, is the disinfecting agent and is referred to as free available chlorine. Since chlorine is an oxidising agent it reacts with all compounds in water which can be oxidised, e.g. converting nitrites to nitrates, or sulphides to sulphates. It also reacts with ammonia to form chloramines. Thus when chlorine is added to water there is an immediate chlorine demand which must be satisfied before a residual of chlorine exists for disinfection.

The formation of chloramines is as shown below:

$$NH_3 + HOCl \rightarrow H_2O + NH_2Cl \text{ (monochloramine)}$$

$$NH_2Cl + HOCl \rightarrow H_2O + NHCl_2 \text{ (dichloramine)}$$

$$NHCl_2 + HOCl \rightarrow H_2O + NCl_3 \text{ (trichloramine)}$$

The chloramines are disinfectants but not nearly as effective as free chlorine (they may have to be 25 times more concentrated to have the same effect).

Chlorine in compounds such as chloramines is referred to as combined residual chlorine. Although not as effective as free chlorine in disinfection, combined chlorine is less likely to produce objectionable tastes and smells. One reason for this is that combined chlorine does not react with phenols, which may be present, to form chlorophenols. In fact, ammonia is sometimes added to water for this reason.

For disinfection with chlorine, World Health Organisation (WHO) guidelines recommend a minimum free chlorine concentration of 0.5 mg l^{-1} after a contact time of 30 minutes at a pH less than 8, provided that the turbidity is less than 1 NTU (nepholometric turbidity unit). The water leaving the chlorine contact tank is usually discharged with a free residual chlorine concentration of 0.5–1.0 mg l^{-1} to ensure that the water is kept safe throughout the supply and distribution system.

Recently, *ozone* (O$_3$, a blue gas and a very strong oxidising agent) has become popular as a disinfectant, particularly as it is effective against viruses, spores and the protozoan *Cryptosporidium*. Also, ozonation does not produce toxic by-products such as trihalomethanes which can occur with chlorine. In France there are about 600 water treatment plants using ozone as a disinfectant. The drawback with ozone, however, is that it is not possible to have a residual level, as there is for chlorine, to confer protection in the supply and distribution system (O$_3$ rapidly breaks down to oxygen). Hence, after ozonation, the water is chlorinated before it goes into the supply system. The ozone used in water treatment plants is usually generated by passing dry air or oxygen between plates, across which a high voltage is imposed. It is expensive to produce.

Ultraviolet radiation can also be used to disinfect water but care must be taken to ensure that no suspended solids are present which could shield the microorganisms and prevent them being destroyed. UV systems are generally only used in small-scale water treatment units. UV is effective against viruses.

SAQ 13

List the advantages and disadvantages of chlorine and ozone as disinfecting agents.

see answer for notes

4.8   Additional treatment

As a result of the stricter standards set by the EC Directive on the Quality of Drinking Water, it is now often necessary for drinking water to have further treatment.

4.8.1   Nitrate removal

Nitrate in water has become a significant problem and the Drinking Water Directive sets a maximum admissible concentration of 50 mg l^{-1}. High nitrate levels can cause cyanosis or methaemoglobinaemia in babies (see Units 5–6).

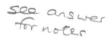

Ion exchange is used in some treatment plants to remove nitrates from drinking water. In this process the water is passed through an ion exchange resin which removes the problem ions and replaces them with ions which do not affect the water quality. At first ion exchange was carried out with zeolites which are naturally occurring insoluble sodium aluminosilicates. Zeolites were able to exchange sodium ions for other ions such as Ca^{2+} and Mg^{2+} which are responsible for water hardness. Artificial zeolites such as permutit are now produced. If the cation exchange sodium resin is represented by Na$_2$R where R is the complex resin base, then the reaction for water softening is

$$Mg^{2+} + Na_2R \rightarrow MgR + 2Na^+$$

$$Ca^{2+} + Na_2R \rightarrow CaR + 2Na^+$$

The treated water then becomes richer in sodium and, unless the water was particularly hard, this is less of a problem.

When all the sodium ions in the exchange resin have been replaced, the resin can be regenerated by passing a strong solution of sodium chloride through it:

$$MgR + 2NaCl \rightarrow Na_2R + MgCl_2$$

As mentioned above, the ion exchange technique is now used to remove nitrate ions from waters which are high in nitrate and do not meet the EC standards for drinking water. In this instance the exchange is with R*Cl where R* is another complex resin base:

$$R*Cl + NaNO_3 \rightarrow NaCl + R*NO_3$$

The ion exchange vessels are taken out of service sequentially for regeneration using a brine solution which displaces the captured nitrate ions.

Ion exchange is also used to reduce the hardness of a water (for example, the small units available for the home) by removing chloride and sulphate ions from water. It can also be used as a ***desalination*** system to reduce the salt content of a water. Small-scale ion-exchange units are commonly used in laboratories to produce pure water called deionised water, an alternative to distilled water.

Biological fluidised beds have also been used to effect nitrate removal. The denitrifying (nitrate-removing) bacteria are grown in an anaerobic environment on the surface of solid particles which are fluidised by the nitrate-containing water. When a carbon source, typically methanol, is added, the bacteria reduce the nitrate in the water to nitrogen gas. Due to the large surface area of the support particles, the biomass concentration is very high (15 000–40 000 mg l^{-1}), leading to rapid rates of denitrification.

As mentioned in Units 5–6, Section 5.7, legislation allows the designation of 'nitrate sensitive areas' and these help to prevent nitrate levels in natural waters increasing in affected areas.

4.8.2   Removal of trace organics

see
set
book

After conventional treatment a water may still contain trace concentrations of synthetic organic compounds which if left in the water can lead to taste and odour problems. The problem is most likely to arise where the raw water abstracted has been badly polluted. The problem can be solved by including the process of granular ***activated carbon*** adsorption after the filtration process. Granular activated carbon (GAC) can be obtained from roasting vegetable or animal matter at 800–900 °C in a vacuum furnace. It is extremely porous, having a high surface area per unit mass (up to 1000 square metres per gram). GAC is therefore an effective adsorbent of organic compounds. Its effectiveness can be measured by the reduction in the chemical oxygen demand (COD) and the total organic carbon of the water. GAC can be used for the removal of soluble phenols which would produce strongly smelling and tasting chlorophenols upon reaction with chlorine in the disinfection stage. In the event that trihalomethanes are formed after disinfection by chlorine, GAC can be used to eliminate these toxic compounds. GAC, once exhausted, can be regenerated by heat treatment.

Another method of removing trace organics is to oxidise them to harmless products such as CO_2 by using ozone, which is a very strong oxidising agent. Ozone and activated carbon are capable of removing trace quantities of organics present in water. Investigations were under way in 1992 (e.g. by Thames Water) on the use of these substances for the reduction of pesticide levels in raw water supplies to 0.1 ppb to comply with the limit specified by the EC.

SAQ 14

Which of the following is true?

A   There are three [4] important zones in a sedimentation tank, namely, the inlet zone, the settling zone and the outlet zone. + sludge zone

B   Flocculent particles will reach the base of a settlement tank ahead of discrete particles. False, other way round

C   For a surface loading of 30 m³ m^{-2} d^{-1}, in a sedimentation tank with floor dimensions 14 m × 50 m, the maximum flow rate allowed is 2.4 m³ s^{-1}. 0.24 m³s^{-1}

D   It is the positive [−ve] charge carried by colloidal articles and microorganisms that prevents them from aggregating and settling.

E   An ion exchange resin to remove nitrate from water can be represented as NaR R*Cl
     where R is the complex resin base.

✓ F   Free available chlorine is a disinfection agent and is present in water as HOCl,
       hypochlorous acid.

4.9   *Fluoridation*

The addition of this process to water treatment has caused much controversy and public debate. The problem seems to be that many see the addition of fluoride to drinking
water as the addition of a poison, and others see it as the use of mass medication
whether the individual wishes it or not. The 'mass medication' lobby claim that indi-
viduals should have the right to choose if they want to ingest fluorides and if they do
wish this then they can use fluoride toothpaste or tablets.

Many waters do, however, have a natural fluoride content (Figure 23) and it has been
suggested that the presence of fluoride in a concentration of 1.0 mg l^{-1} is beneficial in
preventing dental decay. Above this concentration there is the likelihood of 'mottled
teeth' occurring. The EC Drinking Water Directive does allow higher concentrations
than the MAC value of 1.5 mg l^{-1} if the fluoride is natural to the water.

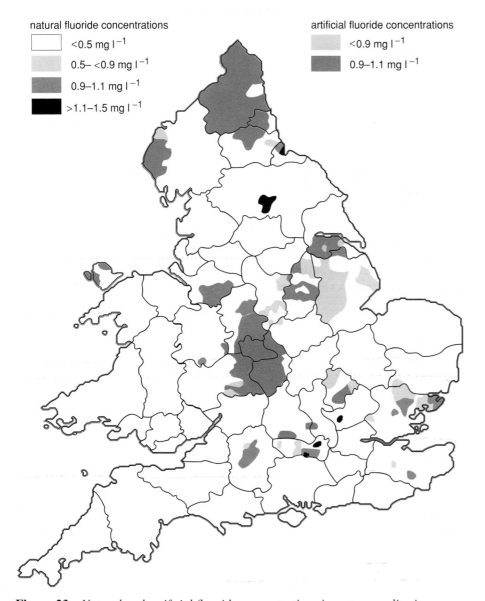

natural fluoride concentrations

☐ <0.5 mg l^{-1}

   0.5– <0.9 mg l^{-1}

   0.9–1.1 mg l^{-1}

■ >1.1–1.5 mg l^{-1}

artificial fluoride concentrations

   <0.9 mg l^{-1}

   0.9–1.1 mg l^{-1}

Figure 23 *Natural and artificial fluoride concentrations in water supplies in
England and Wales.*

Fluoride is added to the water as the last process in water treatment. There are three commonly used chemicals:

1   sodium fluorosilicate (Na_2SiF_6);
2   sodium fluoride (NaF);
3   fluorosilicic acid (H_2SiF_6).

In water, all these chemicals dissociate to give fluoride ions, e.g.

$$SiF_6{}^{2-} + 2H_2O \rightarrow 4H^+ + 6F^- + SiO_2$$

The three fluorides must be handled carefully during their addition to the water as they are harmful if they are inhaled, ingested or come into contact with the skin. It must, however, be remembered that the addition of chlorine to water is readily accepted and chlorine is a poisonous gas!

Exercise

A natural water contains 0.55 mg l^{-1} of fluoride ion and is to be treated with sodium fluoride so that the final concentration will be 1.0 mg l^{-1} of fluoride ion. The flow of water to be treated is 1000 litres per second. Calculate the daily weight of sodium fluoride that will be required.

Answer

The fluoride ion to be added is the difference between the required concentration and the natural concentration, i.e.

$$1.0 - 0.55 = 0.45 \text{ mg } l^{-1} \text{ F}^-$$

The molecular weight of sodium fluoride = 23 + 19 = 42

Therefore, to add 0.45 mg of F^- will require

$$0.45 \times \frac{42}{19} = 0.9947 \text{ mg of NaF}$$

This amount is required for 1 litre of water.

Daily water flow = 1000 × 60 × 60 × 24 l

$$= 86.4 \times 10^6 \text{ l}$$

Therefore, amount of NaF required $= \dfrac{0.9947 \times 86.4 \times 10^6}{10^6}$ kg

$$= 85.94 \text{ kg}$$

4.10   Plumbo-solvency

Many *water supplies* in the UK are naturally acidic and when this type of water is supplied through lead pipes, the lead dissolves into the water. The Drinking Water Directive has set a maximum admissible concentration of 50 μg l^{-1} lead in water. The obvious solution to this problem is to remove all lead piping but this will be a costly exercise. As an interim measure, the water leaving the treatment works can be dosed with lime or phosphate to increase the pH (making the water less acidic), thus reducing the extent to which the lead dissolves in the water. Another practical measure in the home is to let the water run for a minute or two before using it. This is especially advisable in the morning when the lead concentration in the water may be high because the water has stood in the pipes overnight.

4.11   Sludge treatment and disposal

The sludge collected in the sedimentation tank in the treatment process has to be disposed of. In some instances the wet sludge is transported to the nearest sewage works where it is discharged into the raw sewage inlet channel. The presence of the added chemicals can help in the primary sedimentation of the crude sewage (see next section). Alternatively, the sludge can be sent to a landfill site after it has been concentrated into a cake by dewatering.

The dewatering is carried out by pressure filtration, vacuum filtration or centrifugation. In pressure filtration, the sludge is pressed at high pressure between filter cloths. *Vacuum filters* are a more recent development. They are popular in the USA but few British works employ them. A slowly revolving drum, partly immersed in the sludge, carries a filter cloth through which water is sucked from the sludge under vacuum. In centrifuging, chemically or biologically conditioned sludge falls onto the centre of a rapidly rotating bowl. The solids are thrown to the outer edge of the bowl where they are removed by a scraper. With chemical-conditioned sludge, 80–98% of the solids can be separated. These solids would contain typically 10–35% water.

SAQ 15

1000 kg of hydrofluorosilicic acid (H_2SiF_6) is added per day to a flow of 15000 l s^{-1} to achieve a concentration in the water of 1.0 mg l^{-1} fluoride ion. What was the natural concentration of fluoride in the water?

4.12   Groundwater treatment

The treatment of ground water frequently does not extend beyond disinfection. However, ground water may contain dissolved substances such as carbon dioxide and iron for which additional treatment (aeration, etc.) may be required. In some instances ground water may be hard, and where the concentration of dissolved solids is greater than about 300 g m^{-3} it may be desirable to soften the water to reduce scale formation and soap wastage. The methods usually adopted are precipitation and ion exchange.

4.13   Desalination – not examined

In many parts of the world, surface water or non-saline groundwater stocks are not adequate to satisfy the water demand made by the inhabitants. While one immediately thinks of the Middle East as being one such area, it is not obvious that many islands (e.g. the Canary Isles, Madeira) also suffer the same problem. In such circumstances, people have been forced to consider the sea and brackish underground aquifers as water sources. To make these saline waters potable, the salt has first to be removed by *desalination*. Desalination systems are also used on ships and on offshore oil and gas production platforms as a means of producing potable water. The two major desalination processes used worldwide are multistage flash distillation and *reverse osmosis*. Other techniques commonly used are electrodialysis and solar distillation.

4.13.1   Multistage flash distillation

In this process (Figure 24) saline water (screened first, if it is sea water) is distilled under reduced pressure in a series of sealed tanks. Due to the reduced pressure, the water evaporates suddenly or 'flashes' at a temperature lower than 100 °C, typically 80 °C. Pure water condenses on cooling coils in the tanks and is collected. As the temperature of the feed water falls in each succeeding tank (as the latent heat of evaporation is extracted from it) a correspondingly lower pressure has to be maintained for flashing off to occur.

Multistage flash (MSF) units are often located alongside power generation plants in order to utilise the waste heat generated in them. MSF plants can suffer from scale deposition and corrosion. Scale deposits of, for example, $CaCO_3$ and $Mg(OH)_2$ can interfere with the transfer of heat between different parts of the process, and can increase the resistance to fluid flow due to an increase of surface friction. Scale deposition is usually prevented by the addition of scale inhibitors to the feed. These modify the crystal structure of the scale and prevent it building upon surfaces.

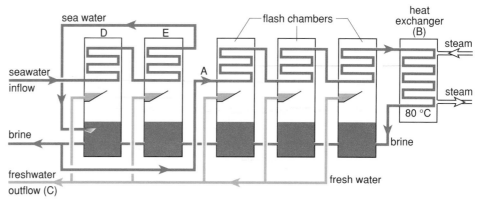

Figure 24   *The multistage flash-distillation process. Brine at (A) passes under pressure in the condenser coils of the flash chambers to heat exchanger (B), and as it flows in the reverse direction, water vapour flashes off and is condensed on the cooler brine-filled coils above. The condensate forms part of the freshwater outflow at (C). The brine, now at 60°C, passes into flash chambers D and E, which contain condenser coils fed with raw sea water. This is recycled into the concentrated brine of the last flash chamber and the resultant liquid is partly run off as waste and partly recycled to A. From right to left, the flash chambers operate at a progressively reduced temperature and pressure.*

Corrosion is another problem experienced in MSF plants. It can be prevented by cathodic protection. This involves the use of a suitable substitute metal which, by acting as an anode, corrodes preferentially in place of the part of the MSF plant at risk.

Sulphate-reducing bacteria, often present in sea water, can contribute to corrosion. Under anaerobic conditions these bacteria reduce sulphate ions to hydrogen sulphide, which in turn dissolves away iron, forming iron sulphide. This results in 'pitting' corrosion. Other bacterial species can oxidise the H_2S to sulphuric acid, which is very corrosive. Control of all forms of bacterially induced corrosion consists essentially of either eliminating conditions suitable for their growth, or, if this is not practicable, of using biocides to prevent them colonising the parts at risk.

4.13.2   Reverse osmosis

When a solution of salt is separated from pure water by a semi-permeable membrane that permits the passage of pure water but prevents that of the salt, water will tend to diffuse through the membrane into the salt solution, continuously diluting it. This is the phenomenon called osmosis. If the salt solution is in an enclosed vessel, a pressure will be developed by the inflowing water. This pressure in a particular solution is known as the osmotic pressure of that solution. Reverse osmosis is a process in which water is separated from dissolved salts in solution by filtering through a semi-permeable membrane at a pressure greater than the osmotic pressure caused by the dissolved salts in the water (Figure 25). The pressure required increases in direct proportion to the concentration of salts. To separate pure water from sea water requires a pressure of more than 5×10^6 Pa.

Reverse osmosis systems operate at ambient temperature, in contrast to multistage flash distillation. This low temperature operation minimises scaling and corrosion.

The basic components of a reverse osmosis unit are the membrane, a membrane support structure, a containing vessel, and a high pressure pump. Cellulose acetate and nylon are the most commonly used membrane materials. To prevent clogging of the membrane, prior filtration of the feed water is necessary. To decrease scaling potential, iron and manganese removal may also be necessary. The pH of the feed should be adjusted to a range of 4.5–7.5 to inhibit scale formation.

4.13.3   Electrodialysis

Electrodialysis is an electrochemical process in which ion transfer separates salt from water. It is effective only for substances that can be ionised: for example, salt (NaCl)

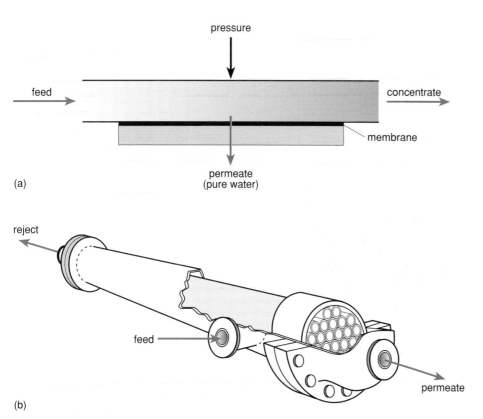

(a)

(b)

Figure 25 *Reverse osmosis membranes in (a) planar and (b) tubular designs.*

becomes, in solution, a mixture of Na^+ and Cl^- ions. (Silica, on the other hand, does not ionise and hence is not removed by electrodialysis. It could, however, be removed by reverse osmosis.) When electrodes, connected to a suitable direct current supply, are immersed in a salt solution, current will flow, carried by the ions. The ions with a positive charge are attracted towards the negative cathode and are called cations. Negatively charged anions flow toward the positive anode. In electrodialysis, filters or membranes selectively impervious to cations or anions, are placed alternately between the electrodes (Figure 26). Cation filters permit the flow of anions but act as a barrier to positively charged cations. Conversely, anions are held back by the anion filter while cations pass through. In certain compartments of the tank, ions will collect as their flow is checked by the appropriate filter. Cells of increasing salt concentration thus alternate with cells of salt depletion. Water sufficiently desalinated is extracted from the appropriate compartments. Electrodialysis is only generally used with brackish waters as it is uneconomic for seawater desalination.

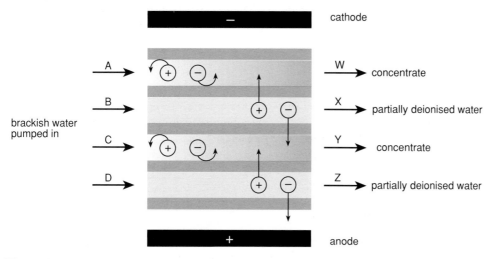

Figure 26 *The principle of electrodialysis.*

4.13.4   Solar distillation

The energy available in solar radiation can be harnessed to distil sea water. In a simple and inexpensive solar still system designed by the Technical University of Athens, for the island of Patmos, sea water is first pumped to a feed reservoir from which it flows by gravity, when required, into a large shallow basin divided into long narrow sections (Figure 27). Separating these channels are concrete strips, which provide access for maintenance. The interior surface of the entire basin is lined with butyl rubber sheet. Above each water-filled section is a double sloping glass roof supported by a light aluminium structure. Heat from the sun passes through the glass, causing evaporation from the seawater surface. The vapour condenses on the inside of the glass and runs down to channels at the edges of the sealed unit along which it travels to the freshwater storage reservoir. The salt concentration in the basin sections grows steadily stronger, and once every two days the resulting brine is run-off to the sea, being then replaced by more sea water. Experience has shown that the 48-hour cycle avoids the formation of scale. As the sun does not shine every day, the designers incorporated a second water channel in the concrete strips. These are fed from the upper surface of the glass panels, and from the concrete itself, when it rains.

The output of distilled water from the Patmos solar still averages three litres per square metre of water surface per day. The only running costs of the system are those of pumping sea water to the feed reservoir, and of general maintenance, which includes cleaning the glass panels.

Desalinated water, without any salts to confer taste, is insipid. It is also corrosive, due to the deficiency of ions which would be present if the water were in its natural state. Lime ($Ca(OH)_2$), phosphates and bicarbonates are added to raise the alkalinity and make the water less corrosive. These chemicals also raise the level of total dissolved solids (TDS) (to about 300 mg l^{-1}), to give the water taste. If unpolluted brackish ground water is available, this can be used instead to raise the TDS level. Often a combination of the two – addition of chemical salts and blending with underground water – is economic. Such a procedure is used in the water supply of Muscat in the Sultanate of Oman. After adjustment of the TDS content, the pH is corrected if necessary. Finally, the water is disinfected and passed into the transmission mains.

4.14   Summary

The basic water treatment process consists of preliminary screening and storage, followed by coagulation and flocculation to allow the aggregation of colloidal particles. Sedimentation of the aggregated particles produces sludge and a partially purified water. The purification process is completed by filtering and finally disinfecting the water before distribution. Some waters may require additional treatment: for example, nitrate removal, or fluoridation, or further removal of organic material by granular activated carbon. The pH may have to be adjusted to minimise plumbo-solvency in areas served with lead distribution pipes. The sludge produced in water treatment can

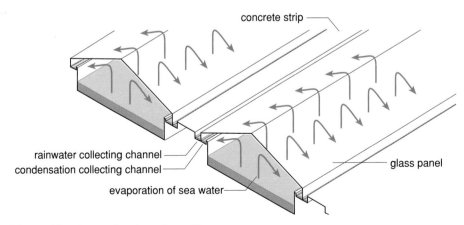

Figure 27   *Principle of a solar still.*

be sent to a sewage works where it can aid primary sedimentation, or it can be dewatered and buried at a landfill site.

In areas of the world lacking adequate quantities of surface water or non-saline ground water, desalination is practised, with the major processes being multistage flash distillation and reverse osmosis.

SAQ 16

List the four commonly used desalination processes for the production of potable water.

5   SEWAGE TREATMENT

5.1   *Introduction*

Water, after use, is discharged as waste. This is usually conveyed by drains and sewers to a treatment plant where the water is cleaned and reused or, as is more usual at the present time, discharged into a receiving water body such as a river. While this is the most popular discharge route, there are some discharges directed into estuaries and the open sea.

Domestic effluent or sewage consists of waste waters from toilets and waste waters (collectively termed 'sullage') from other activities such as bathing, clothes washing, food preparation and the cleaning of kitchen utensils.

In this section we consider the transport of sewage from its point of origin to the treatment plant, and the various processes carried out at the treatment plant to render the sewage innocuous. We begin by considering drains and sewers.

5.2   *Drains*

Drains are pipes or other conduits which convey water away from a building or from an area to prevent it accumulating and causing a nuisance. The water drained from fields, roofs or paved surfaces may be relatively clean. However, the term 'drain' is also used specifically for the pipe which carries foul drainage (the wastes from toilets and washing facilities) to the public sewer.

In a building, waste pipes take the water discharges from various points to the main underground drain (Figure 28). In the UK the pipes above ground are now placed

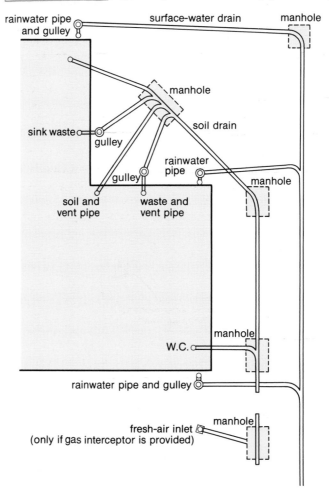

Figure 28   *Drainage system for a house.*

entirely within the building to avoid frost damage. The obvious drainage pipes in your own building will be from the toilets and wash basins. A vertical extension of the waste pipe, opening at roof level, is often used to ventilate the underground drain in a building. Such a vent reduces air pressure fluctuation, prevents the build-up of offensive smells within the drain, and aids the drying and subsequent flaking-off of deposits from the drain walls. Smells from drains were once regarded as a principal health hazard. You will realise that this is not true, but that ventilation is retained as a consideration of amenity as well as for the practical reasons mentioned.

Gutters, pipes and drains conveying rain water away from all roofs, roads and paved areas in many new developments, constitute a separate system from that used for sewage. This separation can continue in the sewerage system and subsequent treatment. However, it is often desirable to combine these systems when draining factories and abattoir yards, markets, etc, as these open areas are likely to be sources of pollution. Whether combined or separate, the drainage systems must include a facility for inspection and maintenance and this is provided by manholes or inspection covers. For ease of clearing accidental blockages, drains should always be laid in straight lines between inspection points. This layout should ensure that drain-clearing rods can be introduced when necessary. Although there is no clear rule for the location of inspection points, it has been a tradition to provide inspection chambers at all junctions of drains into which soil pipes discharge. These chambers are also provided at intervals along straight (junctionless) lengths of drain to ensure that the whole length of drain can be 'rodded' satisfactorily.

5.3   Sewers

The flow of sewage from buildings is carried away by drains to the main sewers. These are large pipes or masonry-lined tunnels which convey the combined flow to the treatment works or, in an isolated or coastal area, some other point of disposal.

The primary function of the sewerage system is to maintain a healthy local environment. This includes the avoidance of local flooding and the minimising of river pollution by preventing wastes from running directly into the rivers. Figure 29 shows a typical layout of drains and manholes used to connect a single household to the public sewer. Raw domestic sewage in a fresh state is typically light grey to brown in colour. In it, however, the biodegradation of its organic content is constantly in progress. Provided a measurable amount of dissolved oxygen is maintained in the waste water, the biodegradation process will remain aerobic and the sewage will remain fresh. Should the rate of oxygen demand exceed the rate at which oxygen can be dissolved from the sewer atmosphere, anaerobic conditions will result – the waste water will rapidly turn a black colour and hydrogen sulphide will be formed. Hydrogen sulphide gas evolved in sewers is a hazard to sewer maintenance personnel and is a major cause of corrosion of sewer structures. It also causes severe odour problems in the primary phase

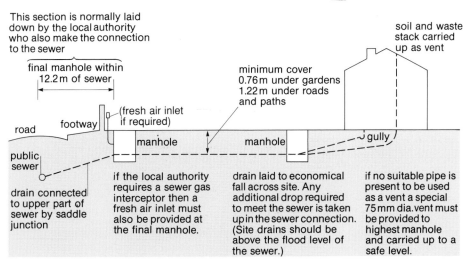

Figure 29   *Drain connections to main sewer.*

of the treatment works. These problems can be particularly severe in hot climates because of the reduced solubility of oxygen at higher temperatures, and the more rapid biological action. Aerobic conditions may be ensured by providing adequate sewer ventilation, by designing sewers with steep gradients and by minimising the total time that sewage remains in the collection system.

A considerable portion of the water supplied to a community does not reach the sewers. This includes water used by manufacturing industries and power plants, and water used in gardening and in actual consumption, i.e. in drinking and cooking. It also includes leakage and water used in extinguishing fires. Not counting groundwater infiltration into sewers, some 80% of the water supplied ends up as waste water in sewers.

> What would you expect the mean sewage flow per household to be (in $m^3 \ d^{-1}$) according to the estimated water demand given in Section 1.3? (Use a figure of 3.5 persons per household.)
>
> For a demand of 140 l $person^{-1} \ d^{-1}$, the mean flow per household would be
>
> $$3.5 \times \frac{140}{10^3} \times \frac{80}{100} = 0.39 \ m^3 \ d^{-1}$$
>
> Of course this flow will be unsteady, matching the demand pattern fairly closely (see Figure 12).

The size of a sewer (or underground drain) is calculated according to the flow that is to be carried.

The ratio of maximum and minimum flow rates varies with position along the sewer lines. In the smaller upstream sewers serving small areas the ratio can be large with wide fluctuations of flow. In the larger downstream sewers leading to the treatment plant, the extremes of flow will be less pronounced, as a result of differing travelling times from the various tributary areas and the attenuation of the maximum and minimum flows.

In addition to flows from household sewage and trade wastes (effluents from industry), surface and ground water will also influence the flow rate. During storms, rainwater run-off entering the sewer can totally dwarf the sewage flow. A properly laid sewer is watertight when laid and installed, but ground movement may cause it to be damaged. If the groundwater level rises above the sewer, water will leak in (or infiltrate). This water is called infiltration water. On the other hand, if the groundwater level falls below the sewer, it is possible for sewage to leak out and contaminate underground water supplies.

The critical factors in calculating surface water discharges are the likely intensity and duration of rainfall, and the area and permeability of the surfaces from which the water is drained – that is, how much soaks in and how much runs off. This was discussed in Section 2.7.

Some coastal communities discharge their sewage directly into the sea from submerged outfalls. The dispersion of the sewage as it rises to the sea surface is analogous to the dispersion of chimney plumes. The extent of dilution depends on the velocity of the jet of sewage leaving the end of the pipe, the depth of water over the outfall and the tidal velocity at this point. After the sewage and entrained sea water reaches the sea surface, it spreads as a layer of less dense material over the dense sea water. Final dispersion occurs by mixing of this layer due to the natural turbulence of the sea.

The combined total of average daily flows due to sewage and trade wastes to be expected in a sewer is called the dry weather flow and other flows may be expressed in terms of this.

5.4 Dry weather flow

Strictly, the **_dry weather flow_** is the rate of flow of sewage and trade waste, together with infiltration, if any, in a sewer in dry weather. This is measured as the average flow during seven consecutive days without rain, following seven days during which the rainfall did not exceed 0.25 mm on any one day. Preferably, the flows during two periods in the year, one in summer and one in winter, should be averaged to obtain the average dry weather flow.

The dry weather flow (DWF) may also be calculated using the following formula:

$$DWF = PQ + I + E$$

where

> P is the population served;
>
> Q is the average daily per capita domestic wastewater generation ($m^3 \, d^{-1}$);
>
> I is the average rate of infiltration ($m^3 \, d^{-1}$);
>
> E is the average volumetric flow rate of industrial effluent discharged to sewers ($m^3 \, d^{-1}$).

(For practical purposes, Q is taken to be equal to the domestic water consumption.)

The dry weather flow is used in determining the capacity of the treatment works, typically specified as capable of treating up to three times DWF. Allowance is usually made for a further three times DWF to be treated for gross solids and grit removal only. This is to cater for storm waters.

5.5 Gravity flow

Almost all drainage systems are based on gravity flow and partially filled pipes. Foul drains and sewers slope downwards towards the treatment works or pumping stations, and the sewage flows in the bottom of the pipe rather than filling it completely. For example, foul drains are designed to contain flows to a depth of three-quarters of their diameter. With a sudden discharge, the level in the pipe rises, so the surge is stored temporarily and may flow away over a longer period.

Partially filled gravity sewers possess several advantages over pipes designed to be operated completely full for most flows. This follows particularly from their 'self-cleansing' operation, since, when designed properly, sewage is not delayed in transit, as it would be at low flow rates in full pipes. Further advantages are:

1   The maintenance of higher velocities at low flows results in less deposition of material and the sewage arrives at the sewage works 'fresher' than it would otherwise be, the organic matter having undergone relatively little decomposition.

2   At normal flows, maintenance work can be carried out in the sewers.

3   No power is needed for pumping.

Although local authorities have their own requirements for minimum gradient, the larger the diameter that is chosen for the sewer, the less steep the fall that is required. The slope must be sufficient to provide a flow of water fast enough to sweep the solids along. A minimum self-cleansing velocity of 0.6 to 0.75 m s⁻¹ is needed to avoid stranding solid matter and the system should be designed so that this velocity is achieved at least once per day. The depth of flow is important since this affects not only the velocity of flow, but the area inside the sewer that is cleansed. Moreover, the minimum gradients cannot be calculated by assuming that the drains or sewers are perfectly positioned. Irregularities of laying, ground movement and distortion of pipes mean that steeper gradients are needed in practice than would be proposed for ideal conditions. Occasionally, when flows in an existing foul sewer are low and give problems of adequate self-cleansing, it is common practice to supplement the flow with rainwater run-off by connecting in some roof or road gutter flows to the sewer.

It is not always possible to design drainage and sewerage systems to allow effluent to flow under gravity all the way from its source to the treatment works. The difference in height between the drainage area and the treatment works may be insufficient or the topography might be unsuitable. For these circumstances it is necessary to pump the effluent to the works, i.e. to use a rising main.

SAQ 17

Which of the following factors can be used to explain the difference between a sewer and an underground drain?

 *see answer*

A   Size
B   Gravity flow
C   Pipe material
D   Jointing

SAQ 18

Which of the following parameters would you expect to differ between a rising sewer main and a gravity sewer of the same discharge flow rate? How will they differ?

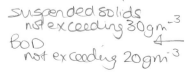 *All differ except C — see answer*

A   Diameter
B   Pressure
C   Type of effluent
D   Gradient
E   Speed of flow

SAQ 19

Estimate the maximum sewage flow rate to a treatment plant serving a population of 20000. Assume that infiltration accounts for 20% of DWF and that the total per capita water consumption (domestic and industrial) is 250 litres per person per day, of which 80% enters the sewer.

5.6   Functions of sewage treatment

About 96% of the population of the UK is served by a sewer network which transports their wastes away for disposal. Most of the sewage is treated in sewage works before discharge into rivers or the sea. There are instances of direct discharge of untreated sewage but many of these will be eliminated with the implementation of the EC Directive on Urban Waste Water Treatment (see Units 5–6, Section 5.6). The remaining 4% of the UK population, mainly in rural areas, use septic tanks or small-scale package treatment plants (described later) to dispose of their sewage.

The functions of sewage treatment are:

1   to reduce the total biodegradable material, including suspended solids, to acceptable levels as measured by BOD and suspended solids concentrations;

2   to remove toxic materials;

3   to eliminate pathogenic bacteria.

Figure 30 shows a typical sewage treatment plant designed to produce a '30/20' effluent.

---

suspended solids not exceeding 30 g m^{-3}
BOD not exceeding 20 g m^{-3}

SAQ 20

What is a '30/20' effluent?

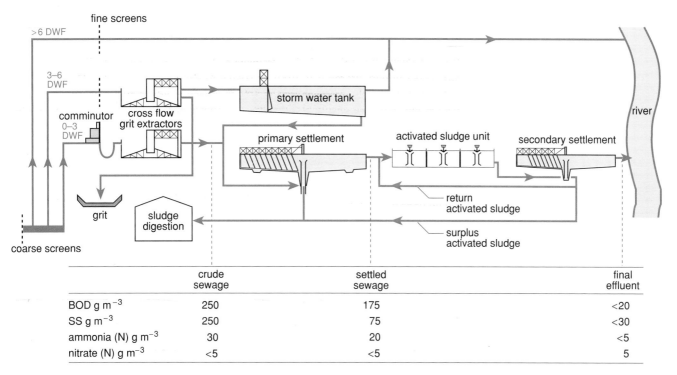

	crude sewage	settled sewage	final effluent
BOD g m^{-3}	250	175	<20
SS g m^{-3}	250	75	<30
ammonia (N) g m^{-3}	30	20	<5
nitrate (N) g m^{-3}	<5	<5	5

Figure 30 *Diagram of a typical sewage treatment plant, designed to produce a '30/20' effluent.*

A typical sequence of treatment is as follows:

1 *Preliminary treatment*

    (a) Removal of gross material by screening.

    (b) Shredding of paper and rags by comminutors (rotating, slotted drums equipped with cutting blades – detailed in the next section).

    (c) Removal of grit.

2 *Primary treatment*

    Removal of fine solids by settlement.

3 *Secondary treatment*

    (a) Biological oxidation of organic matter.

    (b) Removal of solids produced by biological treatment.

If operating as designed, the quality of effluent after secondary treatment should be of '30/20' standard, i.e. with a suspended solids content not exceeding 30 g m^{-3}, and a biochemical oxygen demand not exceeding 20 g m^{-3}.

The quality of the secondary effluent can be improved by further tertiary and advanced wastewater treatment.

4 *Tertiary treatment*

    Reduction of the suspended solids content and the BOD concentration still further, typically to 10 g m^{-3} of each. Removal of N, P and ammonia.

5 *Advanced wastewater treatment*

    Removal of trace quantities of organics. Disinfection.

The products of sewage treatment are:

- an effluent of acceptable quality in relation to the receiving watercourse;
- sewage sludge.

In practice, it is not considered sensible to treat all the waste water entering a sewage works at all times. We have seen that the flow in the sewer or rising main reaching a sewage works can fluctuate a great deal. To provide a treatment capacity for the maximum flow would mean that much equipment would be idle for long periods. Experience has shown that a plant capacity that can treat three times the dry weather flow is a reasonable compromise.

All sewage treatment works are provided with a safety device to avoid the plant being damaged by excessive flows. It is called the storm overflow and its function is to cause the excess flow over the treatment capacity to bypass the works. Typically, a trunk sewer carries the overflow to an open channel near the river serving as the receiving body. The side of the channel nearer to the river is lower than the other so that when the flow in the channel reaches the maximum capacity the mixture of storm water and sewage spills over it. There another channel leads through coarse screens to the river.

> Can you think of a reason why this treatment would not be sufficient for storm water?

When a storm occurs, the early part of the storm cleanses the roads and streets, and also flushes out the combined sewer system where a certain amount of sedimentation has taken place. Thus the early flow of a storm can be considerably contaminated by oil and other materials from roads which have settled in the sewers; even in a river swollen by the storm it could prove to be a problem. To overcome this, sewage works also have storm tanks. These tanks, in series, are filled with the contaminated early storm flow and only when they are full can the now less-polluting storm water reach the river. In many instances the full capacity of the storm tanks is not reached during any one storm, so when the flow reduces, the storm tanks are emptied by pumping their contents back to the beginning of the treatment process. Under these circumstances no untreated sewage can reach the receiving water.

SAQ 21

What problems for sewage treatment are posed by a combined sewerage system?

5.7   Preliminary treatment

The processes of screening, comminution (see below) and grit removal used in preliminary treatment remove the larger floating and suspended matter. They do not make a significant contribution to reducing the pollution load but they do make the sewage easier to treat by removing material which could cause blockages or damage equipment. The screenings may be burnt in an on-site incinerator or buried in a landfill site. Raking of the screens on many small sewage works is still done manually – a job not many people like to do. Even if automatic raking is incorporated, the movement and disposal of screenings is a very unpleasant task.

Screening does not remove small stones or grit which will be present. These abrasive materials increase the rate of wear of mechanical plant and can also settle easily, causing blockages in pipes.

These abrasive substances (which often include pieces of metal and glass) are usually removed in a parabolic-shaped grit channel (Figure 31) where the sewage flow is reduced to 0.3 m s^{-1} to allow the grit to settle by gravity. This velocity does not allow the (lighter) organic material to settle and this material is carried forward. The grit deposited in the grit channel is removed daily using manual and/or mechanical methods, and put into a skip for disposal, usually at a landfill site. Other types of grit removal systems, apart from grit channels, are available. In the cylindrically shaped Pista grit trap (Figure 32) centrifugal action is used to enhance separation of the grit. In the crossflow grit extractor (Figure 33), grit-laden sewage flows into a large square tank at a velocity less than 0.3 m s^{-1}. This allows fine grit also to settle. In addition, some organic solids settle out. In this system, the grit is collected and washed before disposal. It can be used for road gritting if it is thoroughly washed. The wash waters containing the organic matter are returned to the sewage inflow downstream of the grit extractor.

device for removing collected grit

skip for transport of grit

grit channels

Figure 31 *Grit channels.*

In some treatment works, coarse screens are followed by comminutors (instead of fine screens). A comminutor consists of a slotted, rotating drum fitted with cutting blades. Sewage with solids passes through the slots into the drum where the solids are macerated. Grit removal then follows. In sewage with a high proportion of grit, to save the comminutor blades from being prematurely worn down, grit removal may precede comminution.

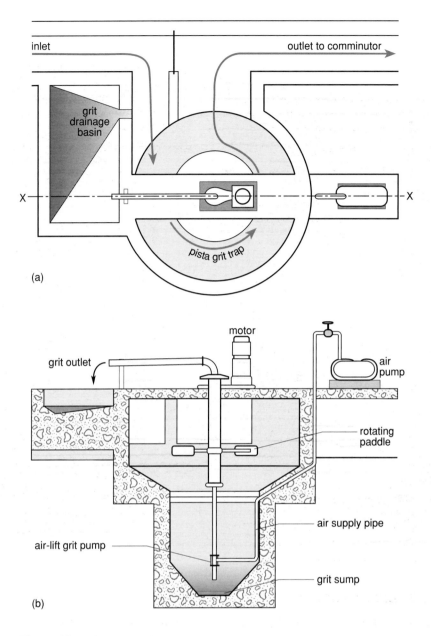

Figure 32   *The Pista grit trap.*

Figure 33 *An empty crossflow grit extractor*

5.8   *Primary treatment*

Now that most of the coarse particles have been removed, only fine particles remain in suspension in the sewage and the next stage in sewage treatment allows the sewage to travel at low velocity through large tanks so that most of the remaining particles can fall out of suspension. This process is called primary sedimentation. The effluent emerging from the primary sedimentation tank is referred to as settled sewage, and the sludge produced is called *primary sludge*.

Primary sedimentation removes approximately 70% of the suspended matter. Because some of these solids are biodegradable, the BOD is also reduced, by some 30% (see Figure 30).

The tanks used in primary sedimentation are similar to those described in Section 4.4 where sedimentation in water treatment was discussed. Thus the tanks could be circular with radial flow, rectangular with horizontal flow, or hopper-bottomed with upward flow. Unlike in water treatment, however, the upward flow tanks usually have their inlet near the surface (Figure 34).

Circular tanks are not as compact as rectangular tanks. Hopper-bottomed tanks are popular on small sewage works where the extra cost of construction is more than offset by the absence of any scraping mechanism which would require maintenance. The sludge obtained from primary sedimentation is drawn off and can be sent on for further treatment (e.g. *anaerobic digestion*) or dewatered before disposal. The problem of sludge disposal will be looked at in Section 6.

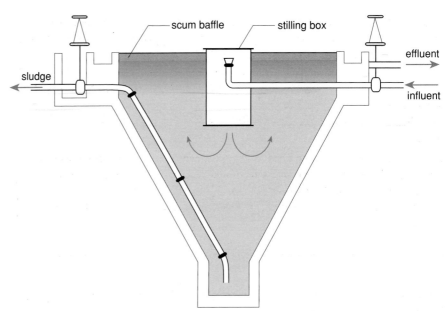

Figure 34   *Upward flow sedimentation tank as used in sewage treatment.*

Retention time in primary sedimentation tanks is generally between 2 and 6 hours and the tanks used have depths of between 2 and 4 metres.

5.9   Secondary (biological) treatment

Before a sewage works can discharge its effluent, the BOD and other polluting factors of the effluent must be reduced. This is achieved by using the process of biological oxidation which uses the same reactions as occur in natural self-purification (see Units 5–6). The main difference in the treatment process compared with natural water purification is that the former attains a higher level of purification through providing optimum conditions.

In *sewage treatment* the two major categories of processes which use biological oxidation are the *activated sludge process* and biological filtration. In drinking water treatment, as we saw in Section 4.6, biological oxidation also takes place to a certain extent in slow sand filters.

The principal parameter in biological treatment is the ratio of food-to-microorganism (F/M) in a process. This can be defined as follows:

$$\text{F/M} = \frac{\text{mass of BOD applied to the biological stage each day (kg BOD d}^{-1})}{\text{mass of microorganisms in the biological stage (kg biomass)}}$$

The F/M ratio is often referred to as the organic loading rate. Figure 35 shows a typical biological growth curve which indicates how the concentration of microorganisms

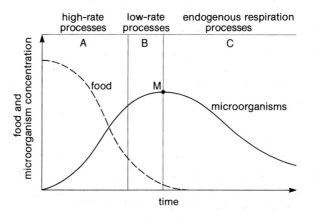

Figure 35   *The biological growth curve.*

(biomass) varies with the food supply. When food supply is present in excess (region A) the growth rate of microorganisms is high. When food supply declines (region B) the rate of organism growth slows down till at point M, with food supply exhausted, the concentration of organisms reaches a maximum. Without food the organisms die and the total cell mass declines (region C). Practical biological treatment processes operate continuously, either in the high growth rate region A with high values of food-to-microorganism ratio (F/M>1.0), or in the low growth rate region B with low values of F/M (<0.1).

Selection of the F/M ratio to be used in the treatment gives the required size of the biological reactor needed, since the size of the reactor will be proportional to the quantity of biomass present. Low-rate processes (low F/M) require a larger quantity of biomass than high-rate processes (high F/M) for the same BOD input and are consequently of a larger size.

Exercise

After sedimentation, a settled sewage with 200 g m^{-3} BOD is to be treated biologically at a flow rate of 2500 m^3 per day.

(a) Calculate the amount of biomass needed if a low-rate process with an organic loading rate of 0.07 kg BOD per kg biomass per day were to be used.

(b) Calculate the amount of biomass needed if a high-rate process with an organic loading rate of 1.8 kg BOD per kg biomass per day were to be chosen instead.

Answer

Mass of BOD added to biological stage per day

$$= \text{flow rate} \times \text{BOD}$$

$$= 2500 \times \frac{200}{1000} \text{ kg d}^{-1}$$

$$= 500 \text{ kg d}^{-1}$$

(a) Biomass = 500/0.07 = 7143 kg

(b) Biomass = 500/1.8 = 278 kg

Another feature of biological systems is the net mass increase in biological solids (sludge). It is not feasible to operate biological processes to produce zero net growth of biological solids because a certain proportion of cell material is always relatively resistant to further degradation. Cells grow and in turn die and are used as food by other organisms, but some poorly degradable cell residues will remain. This increase in organism mass will be larger for high-rate processes than for low-rate processes, since in the high-rate region (see Figure 35) a large fraction of the food supply is used for increasing total cell mass. In the low-rate region, the limited food supply tends to be used mostly for sustaining the energy requirements of the cells, with little increase in total cell mass. The implication of these phenomena is that high-rate biological treatment processes impose larger demands for the withdrawal and disposal of sludge resulting from the net mass increase of biological solids.

There are two principal methods of bringing the microorganisms into contact with the effluent. In *biological filters* the active mass of microorganisms grows on a solid support, typically a bed of loose material. In activated sludge systems the microorganisms are suspended in the waste water.

5.9.1   Biological filters

In the early days of sewage treatment the sewage was allowed to 'soak away' through large areas of land and this gave rise to the term 'sewage farm'. It was found, however, that about ten times the volume of sewage could be treated if the sewage was passed through a granular medium of stone or clinker in a biological filter.

Biological filters can be circular (Figure 36) or rectangular in shape and are also known as percolating filters, trickling filters or bacteria beds. They operate by oxidation and not by filtration. The rectangular shape tends to be used in large works to reduce the land area required. The principal idea is that the settled sewage is slowly sprayed over the surface of the stone or clinker so that it is able to trickle down. In this way oxidising bacteria on the media are able to come into contact with the organic constituents of the sewage and oxidation can take place. These bacteria are able to use the ample supply of atmospheric oxygen as long as the material in the beds has a large surface area and the beds are well ventilated. The process contains five important parts:

1   a dosing system or distributor for applying the settled sewage;

2   a filter bed in which the oxidation takes place;

3   an under-drainage system for collecting the treated effluent;

4   a ventilation system to provide oxygen;

5   a sedimentation tank to remove biological solids washed through the filter media.

Figure 36   *A biological filter.*

1   The *dosing system* or distributor sprays the settled sewage over the surface of the bed. Circular beds use a rotating arm distributor. Here the settled sewage enters at the central column of the filter and is discharged through nozzles spaced along low tubular arms which are supported by the central column. The column and the arms rotate slowly parallel to the surface of the bed and so distribute the sewage evenly over the whole surface. In rectangular filters the distributor sprays the settled sewage across the width of the bed and moves slowly down the length of the filter.

2   The *filter bed* must have an adequate depth to ensure that the incoming liquid receives sufficient time for the bacteria to act. Usually the depth of the media is greater than 1.2 metres and less than 2.0 metres. The material forming the filter beds must be durable, strong enough to resist crushing, and frost resistant. Hard-burnt clinker, blast furnace slag, gravel or crushed rock can be used. Clinker and slag tend to give the best results.

The ideal filter media should have the following:

(a) a large surface area on which the biomass can grow;

(b) voids which are large enough to allow the growth of the biomass without clogging and also to permit the passage of air;

(c) a structure which will distribute the sewage over all the surfaces of the bed with a maximum of turbulence so that oxygen transfer can take place.

The surface area of the media is an important parameter, and is related to the porosity of the media. Note, however, that a high porosity is an indication of a large exposed surface only if the pores are open and also interconnected. The measurement that is used to compare the suitability of different media for filters is the specific surface area which is defined as the exposed area per unit volume of material.

Media may also be made from plastic sheets, tubes or other shapes, forming regular modular or random patterns (Figure 37). Plastic filter media have the advantage over clinker and slag in that they provide a larger specific surface area, so smaller, lighter and more compact 'packs' may be used for a given flow of sewage. Against this must be set the facts that they are more expensive than conventional filter media and that it is not possible to achieve as high a degree of treatment using them.

Filters can be distinguished by the flow rate of effluent being treated. High-rate filters treat 10–40 m^3 of effluent per m^2 of filter bed area per day. Low-rate filters treat 1–4 $m^3\,m^{-2}\,d^{-1}$. Most high-rate filters use plastic media and can be expected to remove only 15–50% of pathogenic bacteria in the sewage. BOD reduction may be up to 85%. They are most useful for relieving some of the load at an existing overloaded works and for treating certain industrial effluents. Low-rate filters use conventional media and can be expected to remove 99% of the pathogenic bacteria as well as reducing the BOD of the sewage by up to 95%.

As liquid passes through a filter it loses a considerable height. For this reason it is preferable for filters to be built on sloping sites since this allows gravity to assist flow between the different stages. On flat sites it may be necessary to raise the flow to the filter by pumping.

Aerobic bacteria grow as a film on the surface of the media in the filter. The flow of sewage entrains air, and up-draughts circulate through the bed because bacterial decomposition creates temperature differences. The air movement provides oxygen for the bacteria, which break down the organic matter in the settled sewage to provide energy and make new cell material. Some toxic material can be treated at this stage but the overall efficiency of the bacteria is much reduced if any toxic material is present. Bacteria would proliferate and eventually block the filter were it not for the activities of other forms of predatory life such as protozoa, worms and fly larvae. These live in the filter and graze on the bacteria. The filter flies, however, tend to be a nuisance during the summer months.

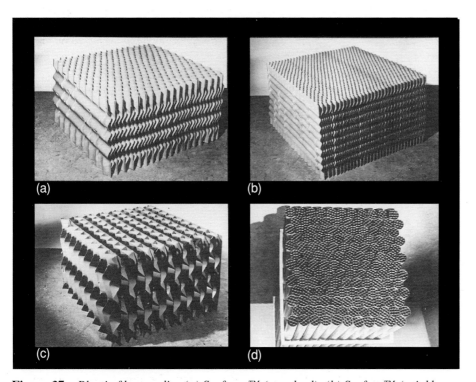

Figure 37 *Plastic filter media: (a) Surfpace™ (standard); (b) Surfpac™ (crinkle-close); (c) Flocor™; (d) Cloisonyle™.*

The microorganisms which make up the gelatinous film at the surface of the filter appear to be made up of three layers: an upper fungal layer, a main algal layer, and a basal layer of algae, fungi and bacteria. The fungi are efficient at oxidising organic matter. The 'blue-green' algae are able to remove nitrogen and minerals. Beneath the surface where there can be no sunlight, algae are absent. Protozoa remove any free-swimming bacteria which, if present, give the effluent a turbid appearance. Biological filtration produces high levels of nitrate. Nitrification occurs from the bacterial action of *Nitrosomonas* and *Nitrobacter* (discussed in Unit 2).

Some bacterial cell material is shed and discharged from the filter with the effluent along with solids which had not settled out in the primary sedimentation tank. This material is known as **humus** and is removed in the final sedimentation tank. The debris which settles out is called humus sludge.

3   The *under-drainage* which collects the effluent is constructed as an impervious base beneath the perforated filter floor. The filter floor slopes towards collecting channels. The under-drainage system should be capable of accommodating the maximum flow rate.

4   As already stated, *ventilation* is achieved by natural air circulation. Sufficient openings are provided at the bottom of the filter to allow air to flow in. In cold climates the air inflow is controlled so that the temperature in the filter does not dip so low as to reduce biological activity.

5   The *sedimentation tanks* used to remove the humus are similar to those used for primary sedimentation. The settled solids are not recycled (unlike in the activated sludge process, discussed later) but are returned to the works inlet where they settle in the primary sedimentation tank.

It is difficult to estimate the total biomass in a biological filter. Although the total surface area of the media gives some indication of the amount of biomass that could be supported, the active mass cannot be easily determined. so it is customary to take the volume of the bed as the most practical measure of biomass and to express the organic loading rate as the BOD applied per day per unit volume of filter medium. If Q is the sewage flow rate in $m^3 \, d^{-1}$ distributed over a filter of cross-sectional area $A \, m^2$ and bed depth H m, and if the BOD of the influent is $Y \, kg \, m^{-3}$ (not $g \, m^{-3}$),

$$\text{organic loading rate} = \frac{(Q)(Y)}{(A)(H)} \text{ kg BOD } m^{-3} \, d^{-1}$$

Exercise

A biological filter for the treatment of the sewage from a small group of houses in a remote area in the countryside has a diameter of 2.5 m and a depth of 2 m.

If the filter each day treats 5 m^3 of sewage with a BOD_5^{20} of 210 g m^{-3} after primary settlement, what is the organic loading rate?

Answer

Organic loading rate $= \dfrac{(Q)(BOD)}{(A)(H)}$ kg BOD $m^{-3} \, d^{-1}$

where

$Q = 5 \, m^3 \, d^{-1}$

$BOD = 0.21 \, kg \, m^{-3}$

$\pi r^2 = \pi (1.25)^2$

$H = 2 \, m$

$\therefore$ organic loading rate $= \dfrac{(5)(0.21)}{\pi \, (1.25)^2(2)}$ kg BOD $m^{-3} \, d^{-1}$

$= \dfrac{1.05}{9.82}$ kg BOD $m^{-3} \, d^{-1}$

$= 0.11$ kg BOD $m^{-3} \, d^{-1}$

In the UK it has been customary to use low-rate filters in a single pass (Figure 38a) in which the sewage is applied at the top and treated effluent discharged at the bottom. This reduces the BOD by 90–95% to produce an effluent of '30/20' standard.

High-rate filters have organic loading rates which are significantly higher than those of low-rate filters. In order to achieve the necessary higher flow rates through the filter, alternatives to the single-pass system have been introduced.

1   The settled filter effluent is recirculated: purified effluent, which has passed through the filter once, is added to the inflowing settled sewage, thereby diluting it up to a maximum flow depending on the speed of action of the filter (Figure 38b).

2   A number of filters are used in series: for example, two filters are used in series with first and second stage settling tanks. Settled sewage is applied at a high rate to the primary filter, and its effluent, after settlement, is passed to the secondary filter (double filtration) and then to the second settling tank. After a period of operation the flow of sewage is changed so that the first stage filter becomes the second and vice versa. This is known as alternating double filtration (Figure 38c).

Both of the above systems enable a greater volume of sewage to be applied to a given volume of medium than with a single-pass filter. Indeed, in an alternating double filtration system up to 20 times the normal loading can be applied to the primary high-rate filter as a partial treatment stage, resulting in a reduction of up to 70% of the BOD.

Table 6 gives typical values of parameters for biological filters.

Table 6   *Typical design values for biological filters*

Filter type	Organic loading/ (kg BOD m^{-3} d^{-1})	Depth of filter medium /m	Effluent SS/BOD (g m^{-3})
Low-rate	0.07–0.3	1.5–2	30/20
High-rate	up to 1.0	1–2	30/30 and greater
High-rate plastic media	1.8	several metres	BOD removal 60–70%
Alternating double filtration	0.24	2	30/20

High-rate filters have a relatively low capital cost and they are easy to install. For this reason they are being considered for the treatment of crude sewage (i.e. before screening and primary sedimentation). The main problems with high-rate filters occur with the disposal of the resulting sludge.

Alternating the filters for double filtration is needed because the first filter becomes organically overloaded, i.e. the organic loading rate becomes too high. Overloading of filters may be indicated by *ponding* – a situation in which the bacterial growth on the media becomes so thick that the air spaces are blocked and the settled sewage is unable to trickle through, causing 'ponds' on the surface. By regularly alternating the first and second stage filters the bacterial growth is never allowed to build up to such an extent.

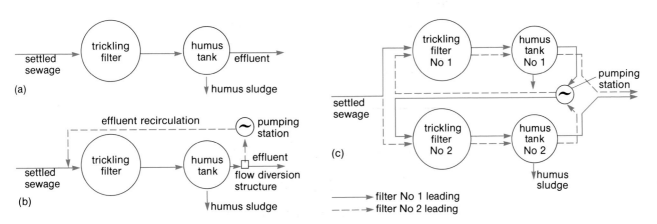

Figure 38   *Flow arrangements for biological filters: (a) single pass; (b) recirculation; (c) alternating double filtration.*

SAQ 22

Which of the following statements are false?

A   Comminutors are always placed after coarse screens but before grit removal in the preliminary treatment of sewage. ✗ *where high grit content Comminutors come after grit removal*

B   In a biological filter nitrification takes place due to the bacterial activity of *Nitrosomonas* and *Nitrobacter*.

C   One advantage of using biological filters is that they ~~do not~~ require ~~final sedimentation tanks~~. *final humus settling tanks*

D   In a biological filter bacteria and algae reduce the BOD of the settled sewage. ✗

E   In alternating double filtration, treated effluent from the primary filter is fed to the secondary filter. When the primary filter shows signs of overloading, the position of the filters in the process is reversed.

SAQ 23

Which of the following considerations is most important (apart from cost) in choosing a medium for a filter?

A   Whether the medium is to be used in a high-rate or a low-rate filter.

B   Whether the filter is to be used for crude sewage or a sewage that has been partially treated by screening and primary sedimentation.

C   The ratio of surface area to unit volume of the filter medium.

D   Regularity of shape of the particles of the medium.

E   Size of the particles of the medium.

SAQ 24

A settled sewage flow of 1200 m^3 per day with 180 g m^{-3} BOD is applied to a low-rate biological filter of 40 m diameter and 1.8 m depth. What is the organic loading rate? What is the rate of removal of BOD in kg per day if the outlet BOD is 20 g m^{-3}?

5.9.2   The activated sludge process

This process was developed in Manchester in 1913–14. It has become extremely popular in sewage treatment as it occupies less space than a biological filter and it has proved useful for treating organic industrial wastes which were once thought to be too toxic for biological treatment. The activated sludge process produces a flocculent, microbial culture which is easily settled. The process (Figure 39) has the disadvantage of being more costly due to its demand for power and maintenance.

The process consists of the following elements:

(a)   an aeration tank;

(b)   an aeration system;

(c)   a final sedimentation tank;

(d)   a return activated sludge system;

(e)   a system to remove the excess activated sludge produced.

Air is introduced into the settled sewage as it arrives from primary sedimentation by either bubbling compressed air through the liquid, or by mechanically agitating the liquid surface. (More information on these systems is given in the next section.) The oxygen 'feeds' aerobic bacteria suspended in the sewage. The bacteria use the organic matter in the sewage to form new cell material. The activated sludge unit also contains protozoa which remove the free-swimming non-settleable bacteria and rotifers which remove small biological floc particles, and so help to produce a clear effluent. Protozoa also play an important role in the reduction of pathogenic bacteria, e.g. those that cause diphtheria, cholera and typhoid.

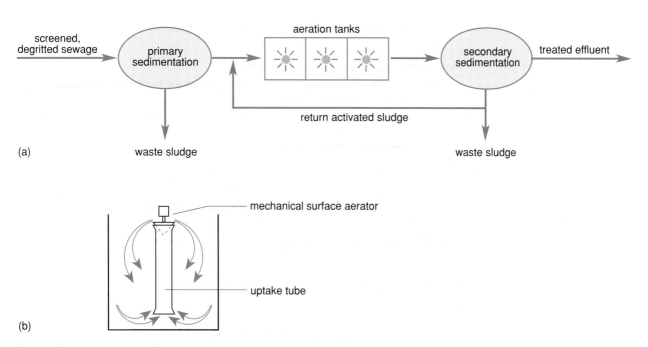

Figure 39 *An activated sludge system, with mechanical aerators: (a) diagram of the process; (b) section through an aeration tank.*

The mixture of sewage and microorganisms in the activated sludge unit is called the mixed liquor. The total suspended solids content determined by filtration and drying is a measure of the microbial mass and the inert substances present, and is referred to as the mixed liquor suspended solids (MLSS). If the MLSS is volatilised at 600 °C any organic fraction will be decomposed to water, oxides of carbon, and ammonia while the inorganic material will remain as oxides, carbonates or other salts. The volatile fraction is referred to as the mixed liquor volatile suspended solids (MLVSS) and gives a closer indication than the MLSS of the biomass in the biological reactor. In routine analysis at treatment plants, it is usually the MLSS that is measured. This is used in calculating the organic loading rate or F/M ratio (see Section 5.9) which is defined as follows:

$$
\begin{aligned}
\text{organic loading rate} &= \text{F/M} \\
&= \frac{\text{mass of BOD applied to the biological stage each day}}{\text{mass of microorganisms in the biological stage}} \\
&= \frac{\text{flow rate (m}^3\,\text{d}^{-1}) \times \text{BOD (kg m}^{-3})}{\text{volume of aeration tank (m}^3) \times \text{MLSS (kg m}^{-3})}
\end{aligned}
$$

Settling is not possible in a liquid which is constantly agitated and so when the treated sewage containing the activated sludge leaves the aeration unit it is allowed to settle in a final sedimentation tank similar in design to that used for primary treatment. The treated effluent from the final settlement tank flows over a weir to be discharged to a watercourse while the sludge settles to the bottom of the tank. A portion of the settled sludge is returned to the aeration unit. This is known as return activated sludge and it is often mixed in the ratio 1:1 with the incoming settled sewage. The settled sludge which is not reused is the surplus sludge and this is usually pumped away for treatment and disposal. It can, however, also be used to aid settling in the primary settlement tank, and is in this case pumped to the inlet of that tank.

It is necessary to maintain a concentration of 1–2 mg l⁻¹ of dissolved oxygen in the mixed liquor. This is particularly important in the final settlement tanks: if there is insufficient oxygen present, the settled activated sludge may go anaerobic before it is returned and this would lead to the death of the organisms present.

The return activated sludge must be present in sufficient volume to give stabilisation in the aeration unit. If insufficient is returned, poor purification will be achieved, and if too much is returned then poor settlement will result in the final settlement tanks.

Because of the importance of maintaining good quality sludge, several indices have been developed to give a guide on sludge quality. Examples are:

1   The sludge volume index (SVI). This can be defined as the volume occupied by sludge containing 1 g of solids (dry weight) after 30 minutes' settlement.

$$SVI = \frac{\text{settled volume of sludge in 30 mins (ml l}^{-1})}{\text{mixed liquor suspended solids (g l}^{-1})}$$

2   The sludge density index (SDI).

$$SDI = \frac{\text{mixed liquor suspended solids (g l}^{-1}) \times 100}{\text{settled volume of sludge in 30 mins (ml l}^{-1})}$$

Values of SVI vary from 40 to 100 for a good sludge, while sludges which have poor settlement and 'bulk' (see Section 5.9.6) in the final settlement tank have values in excess of 180. For SDI, the figures vary between 2.0 for a good sludge and 0.3 for a poor sludge.

Exercise

The sludge solids in 1 litre of mixed liquor are found to be 1850 mg l^{-1} and settle into a volume of 150 ml.

Find the SVI of the activated sludge.

Answer

$$SVI = \frac{150 \text{ ml l}^{-1}}{1.85 \text{ g l}^{-1}}$$

$$= 81.08$$

The retention time of the activated sludge in the aeration unit is typically 6–8 hours. The sludge is, however, recycled for several days before it is finally removed from the system. The sludge age is a value which tells a great deal about the type of activated sludge plant. The sludge age varies according to the type and strength of sewage to be treated.

The sludge age is the ratio of the mass of cells in the bioreactor to the mass of cells wasted per day.

$$\text{sludge age} = \frac{\text{volume of aeration tank (m}^3) \times \text{MLSS (g m}^{-3})}{\text{flow rate of surplus sludge (m}^3 \text{ d}^{-1}) \times \text{solids concentration of sludge (g m}^{-3})}$$

Exercise

An aeration unit has a volume of 13.5×10^3 m^3, with a mixed liquor suspended solids concentration of 1850 g m^{-3}. Daily, 320 m^3 of surplus sludge with a solids concentration of 7500 g m^{-3} is wasted. What is the sludge age?

Answer

$$\text{Sludge age} = \frac{13.5 \times 10^3 \times 1850}{320 \times 7500} = 10.4 \text{ days}$$

In *extended aeration* systems, the retention time of the effluent in the aeration tank is typically 24–48 hours. The sludge produced in this type of system is highly stabilised (oxidised) and the amount of inert sludge left for disposal is reduced to a minimum.

not examined → ## 5.9.3 *Aeration systems*

The main functions of the aeration system in an activated sludge plant can be summarised as follows:

1   to ensure a continuous and adequate supply of dissolved oxygen for the bacteria;

2   to keep the activated sludge solids in suspension;

3   to mix the incoming sewage and the activated sludge;

4   to remove from solution excess carbon dioxide resulting from the oxidation of the organic matter;

5   to assist the flocculation process by which the smaller particles adhere together to settle out later (in the sedimentation tank).

The two main methods by which activated sludge units are aerated are through: (a) the introduction of air into the waste water through pipes or porous diffusers – called diffused air aeration; and (b) the agitation of the waste water by mechanical means such that air from the atmosphere dissolves in it – called mechanical aeration.

(a) *Diffused air aeration.* In this mode of aeration, there are three categories – coarse, medium and fine bubble aeration. In coarse and medium bubble aeration, air is pumped through open-ended pipes (Figure 40a) or pipes with holes often placed along one side of the aeration tank. As the name implies, large air bubbles are formed, with the aeration efficiency less than that of fine bubbles. A circulation pattern is set up in the tank. In fine-bubble aeration, filtered air is pumped to porous dome diffusers (Figure 40b) usually made of ceramic material. Fine air bubbles (approx 2.0 mm in diameter) are generated. With porous diffusers it is essential that the air supplied is free of dust particles as these can clog the diffusers. The dome diffusers are placed in a network on the base of the aeration tank. Although coarse and medium bubble systems have slightly lower aeration efficiencies than fine bubble systems, their lower cost, easier maintenance and the absence of stringent air purity requirements have made them more popular.

(b) *Mechanical aeration.* Mechanical aerators consist of submerged or partially submerged impellers attached to motors which are mounted on floats or on fixed structures. The impellers agitate the waste water vigorously, entraining air from the atmosphere into the waste water. Partially submerged units, called surface aerators (Figure 40c), are popular. A variant of these is the brush aerator (Figure 40d). This is commonly used to provide both aeration and circulation in oxidation ditches (described in Section 5.9.11). It is also possible to have submerged turbine-sparger systems aerators (Figure 40e). These disperse air which is introduced beneath the impeller, and also mix the tank contents.

For means of comparison, typical oxygen transfer rates for the aeration systems described above are given in Table 7.

Table 7   *Typical oxygen transfer rates for a selection of aeration systems at standard conditions (tap water at 20°C, 101.3 Pa)*

Aeration system	Oxygen transfer rate/(kg O_2 kWh^{-1})
Diffused air	
• fine bubble	1.2–2.0
• medium bubble	1.0–1.6
• coarse bubble	0.6–1.2
Low speed surface aerator	1.2–2.4
Brush aerator	1.2–2.4
Turbine-sparger system	1.2–1.4

Source: Metcalf and Eddy Inc., revised by Tchobanoglous, G. (1987) *Wastewater Engineering: treatment, disposal, reuse* (2nd edn), McGraw-Hill, New York.

It is possible to express the BOD loading of an activated sludge unit in terms of an aeration tank loading rate which is defined as:

$$\text{aeration tank loading rate} = \frac{\text{BOD entering aeration tank per day (kg BOD d}^{-1})}{\text{volume of aeration tank (m}^3)}$$

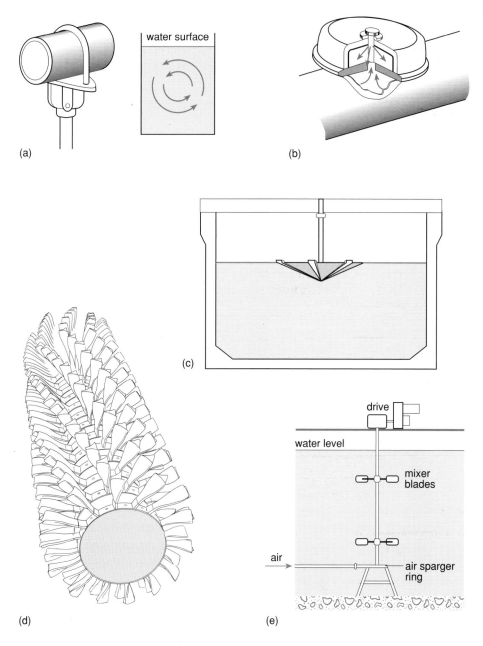

Figure 40   *Various aeration systems: (a) a coarse air diffuser, with water circulation pattern set up in tank; (b) a fine air diffuser; (c) a surface aerator; (d) a brush aerator; (e) a turbine-sparger system.*

5.9.4   *BOD removal in activated sludge units*

Conventional activated sludge processes are 'medium rate' treatment processes with values of organic loading rate (F/M) of about 0.5 kg BOD kg^{-1} MLSS day^{-1}. With an adequate supply of oxygen in the aeration tanks, the rate of BOD removal depends only on the concentration of active microorganisms in the tanks (Figure 41).

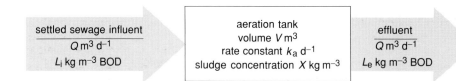

settled sewage influent
Q m^3 d^{-1}
L_i kg m^{-3} BOD

aeration tank
volume V m^3
rate constant k_a d^{-1}
sludge concentration X kg m^{-3}

effluent
Q m^3 d^{-1}
L_e kg m^{-3} BOD

Figure 41   *Mass balance for aeration tank in the activated sludge process.*

That is:

rate of BOD removal (kg day^{-1}) $\propto$ mass of microorganisms or mass of activated sludge

or

$$Q(L_i - L_e) = k_a XV \tag{3}$$

where

L_i is the BOD concentration entering the plant (kg m^{-3})

L_e is the BOD concentration leaving the plant (kg m^{-3})

Q is the sewage flow rate (m^3 d^{-1})

X is the concentration of activated sludge (kg m^{-3})

V is the aeration tank volume (m^3)

k_a is a constant, the activated sludge constant (d^{-1}).

Equation (3) should be compared with the equation for BOD removal in the BOD test (Units 5–6). The BOD test was a batch process, while the activated sludge process is a continuous one. Nevertheless, the biological reactions in both situations are similar.

Exercise

Settled sewage at a flow rate of 1500 m^3 d^{-1} and 200 g m^{-3} BOD is treated in an activated sludge plant which is equipped with an aeration tank 25 m long $\times$ 5 m wide $\times$ 4 m deep and with a sludge concentration $X = 2000$ g m^{-3}. The rate constant $k_a = 0.28$ d^{-1}.

(a) Calculate the overall percentage BOD removal.
(b) Calculate the retention time in the tank.
(c) Calculate the aeration tank loading rate in kg BOD m^{-3} d^{-1}.
(d) Calculate the organic loading rate in kg^{-1} BOD kg^{-1} MLSS d^{-1}.

Answer

(a) From Equation (3)

$$L_i - L_e = \frac{k_a XV}{Q}$$

$$= \frac{(0.28)(2000)(25)(5)(4)}{1500} \text{ g m}^{-3} \text{ BOD}$$

$$= 186.67 \text{ g m}^{-3} \text{ BOD}$$

$$\therefore \% \text{ BOD removal} = \frac{186.67}{200} \times 100$$

$$= 93.3 \%$$

(b) Retention time $t = \dfrac{V}{Q}$

$$= \frac{(25)(5)(4)}{1500} \text{ day}$$

$$= 0.33 \text{ day}$$

(c) Aeration tank loading rate $= \dfrac{QL_i}{V}$

$$= \frac{(1500)(0.2)}{(500)} \text{ kg BOD m}^{-3} \text{ d}^{-1}$$

$$= 0.6 \text{ kg BOD m}^{-3} \text{ d}^{-1}$$

(d) Organic loading rate $= \dfrac{QL_i}{VX}$

$$= \frac{(1500)(0.2)}{(500)(2)} \text{ kg BOD kg}^{-1} \text{ MLSS d}^{-1}$$

$$= 0.3 \text{ kg BOD kg}^{-1} \text{ MLSS d}^{-1}$$

SAQ 25

A litre of activated sludge is found to settle in 30 minutes to a volume of 280 ml, and has a concentration of solids of 1050 mg l^{-1}. What is the SVI of the sludge and is this an acceptable SVI?

SAQ 26

Sewage from a primary settling tank has a BOD of 250 g m^{-3}. It is to be treated in an activated sludge plant to reduce the BOD to 20 g m^{-3}. The aeration tank volume is 250 m^3 and the activated sludge rate constant k_a is 0.3 d^{-1}.

(a) What concentration of active sludge is required in the aeration tank to process 1000 m^3 d^{-1} of sewage?

(b) Suggest what actions might be taken to meet the output BOD specification if, for some reason, the primary treatment fails and the BOD of the sewage entering the activated sludge plant rises to 1000 g m^{-3}?

5.9.5   Secondary sedimentation

The settling tanks in which the activated sludge is separated from the mixed liquor are similar in design to the primary sedimentation tanks. Usually the tanks are circular, and most have floors that slope to the centre, although large tanks have flat floors. In small and medium-sized tanks the sludge is scraped to the centre by helical blades. The sludge then flows through an outlet pipe to the sludge well, from which most of it is pumped back to the aeration tank (the rest being taken away for disposal as surplus sludge). Sludge is removed from flat-floored tanks by suction pipes.

5.9.6   Sludge bulking

The situation can arise in activated sludge plants when the outflow from the activated sludge tank does not settle in the secondary sedimentation tank to produce a sludge and clear water. Instead, the biological flocs remain suspended throughout the sedimentation tank and are carried out in the overflow. The sludge in this situation is referred to as bulking sludge.

Bulking sludge is attributed to two factors:

1   the presence of filamentous organisms or organisms that grow in a filamentous form under adverse conditions;

2   the incorporation of water (bound water) in the bacterial flocs of activated sludge, causing a reduction in the density of the flocs.

Neither the filamentous organisms nor the reduced-density flocs settle easily, resulting in a bulking sludge.

Bulking is caused by fluctuations in wastewater flow and strength, pH and temperature, excessive organic loading, and an inadequate supply of nutrients, e.g. oxygen, N, P, and trace elements.

Remedial measures include adding chlorine or hydrogen peroxide to the sludge recycle stream to eliminate the filamentous organisms. The filamentous organisms, due to their larger surface area, are more affected by these biocides than are the normal activated sludge microorganisms. This is followed by measures to stabilise the inflow and other conditions, e.g. pH, temperature. Steps to reduce the organic loading (e.g. by balancing the inflow, increasing the content of mixed liquor suspended solids to have a favourable F/M ratio) can then be taken. Nutrient addition (e.g. N, P, trace elements such as Fe, Cu, Zn and Mn) may be required.

A lack of dissolved oxygen has been noted more frequently than any other as the cause of bulking. If the oxygen transfer rate with aerators is limited, pure oxygen may be injected into the activated sludge tank to increase the available oxygen. This technique is employed to overcome sludge bulking at the Newbridge Sewage Treatment

Works in Edinburgh where highly polluting organic wastes from a wide variety of food manufacturing and processing establishments constitute a major proportion of the flow treated at the works.

5.9.7   Elimination of pathogens in biological treatment

As we have seen, one of the objectives in treating sewage is the elimination of pathogenic organisms present in the effluent. More than 99% of the pathogenic organisms present in sewage are removed in the treatment process. The pathogens can be grouped broadly into viruses, bacteria and protozoa.

1   *Viruses*. The viruses are usually adsorbed onto bacterial flocs which are in turn removed by sedimentation in the secondary sedimentation tank. Some of the viruses are also consumed by protozoa.

2   *Bacteria*. Bacteria are killed by a number of methods. Some are killed by viruses. Others are consumed by protozoa or are eliminated by toxins produced by other species of bacteria. Many of the pathogenic bacteria are simply enveloped by the rapid growth of non-pathogenic bacteria around them such that they become enmeshed in flocs of non-pathogenic bacteria. The bacterial flocs are then removed in the sedimentation process following biological treatment.

3   *Protozoa*. Most of the protozoa become bound to bacterial flocs which are later removed in sedimentation.

5.9.8   Comparison between activated sludge and biological filter systems

Advantages of the activated sludge process include the following.

1   In the event of a poorer than normal quality influent entering the works, the ability to vary the proportion of sludge that is recycled offers a degree of control over the quality of effluent finally discharged, which is not possible with a normal filter bed.

2   The nuisance of filter flies is avoided.

3   Loss of head through an activated sludge plant is significantly less than that through a filter bed, which may save pumping.

4   Considerable space is saved. Where it is necessary to produce an effluent of particularly high quality, the area of land required for an activated sludge plant is about ten times less than that needed for a conventional filter scheme to treat the same pollution load. For plants required to treat large flows, the smaller area required for activated sludge is the deciding factor. On the other hand, the area required by biological filters is much reduced when high-rate filtration is used, and in recent years the maximum size of new plants that include biological filters has been decreasing.

Disadvantages of activated sludge plants are:

1   They require continuous attention.

2   They consume large amounts of energy and labour – in comparison, the biological filter is simple and requires little attention.

3   They are not tolerant of peak loads, whether of flow or composition.

4   They are noisy in comparison with filters, which can be important when the plant is sited in an area which is otherwise quiet.

5   The annual costs (including operating and maintenance expenses) of the two methods are about the same, but rising energy costs will affect the activated sludge process to a greater extent than filtration methods.

6   Activated sludge systems are more vulnerable than filters to toxic materials present in the influent.

7   Unlike biological filters, the activated sludge process does not convert ammonia to nitrate unless very high concentrations of oxygen are maintained. This requires extra costs and longer retention times in the aeration unit. Nitrification occurs

during the later stages of the biological treatment, i.e. at the bottom of a biological filter and at the 'effluent end' of an activated sludge aeration tank. Nitrification puts a heavy demand on the available dissolved oxygen. Indeed, one of the first signs of overloading of a biological treatment system is the loss of nitrification due to the inability of the system to reach a high enough dissolved oxygen concentration.

5.9.9 Monitoring and control of biological filters

not examined →

Due to the simplicity of biological filter systems, little analysis of the biological stage takes place. The only moving mechanical part is the rotating distributor and this is powered by the incoming wastewater flow. Maintenance of the system consists largely of lubricating the bearings and 'rodding' of the distributor arms to remove any solids that may have come in with the waste water. Excess algal growth (as a result of organic overloading and 'ponding') may occur as sheets blocking the filter bed; these are removed manually using rakes. Organic overloading leads to a loss in nitrification and hence is to be avoided at all cost. The pH of incoming effluent to the plant would be measured to verify that it is within the tolerable range of 6.5–8.0. Analyses would include measurement of the suspended solids content and the BOD values of the final effluent (after secondary sedimentation) to verify compliance with discharge consent conditions. Nitrification may also be monitored. If effective BOD removal were not taking place, it is likely that the incoming BOD, N and P levels would be measured and the N and P levels adjusted, if necessary, to have a BOD:N:P ratio of 100:5:1. This relationship is used as a rule of thumb in the biological treatment of waste water. Alternatively, the presence of toxic compounds might be suspected and these would be sought out and eliminated, preferably at source. BOD data take five days to acquire, so for immediate feedback a measurement of the chemical oxygen demand is often also made and the related BOD value obtained from this using the COD/BOD relationship determined for the particular effluent. Other parameters recorded would be pH, temperature, ammonia-nitrogen content, nitrate-nitrogen content, chloride and the dissolved oxygen level. If metal-bearing effluents were being treated, the concentrations of the metals in the outflow would also be determined. Similar specialist data would be acquired if pesticides, etc. were present in the incoming waste water. The frequency of sampling and analysis would depend on the size of the works. Many of the smaller sewage treatment works would be sampled only weekly or even monthly.

5.9.10 Monitoring and control of the activated sludge process

not examined →

Activated sludge systems are more complex than biological filters and a number of tests are made to monitor the treatment process and to pre-empt any upsets that may occur. Measurements of dissolved oxygen, pH, mixed liquor suspended solids and the sludge volume index are taken. The suspended solids content of the return activated sludge also needs to be measured. Very often process upsets can be detected by a change in the normal colour or smell of the mixed liquor or the return activated sludge. The parameters measured are discussed below.

Dissolved oxygen

The majority of activated sludge plants having dissolved oxygen control systems are controlled by the concentration of dissolved oxygen in the mixed liquor leaving the aeration tank, and a commonly chosen range is 0.5–2.0 mg l^{-1}. Measurements with a portable dissolved oxygen meter can be undertaken to verify that the required level is being maintained.

Mixed liquor suspended solids (MLSS)

The maximum concentration of MLSS which can be achieved depends on the settleability of the sludge and the surface area of the settlement tank. The optimum concentration is usually in the range 2000–3000 mg l^{-1}, though in an aeration tank providing full nitrification it is higher, e.g. 6000 mg l^{-1}. The MLSS concentration in the aeration tank affects the organic loading (F/M) which is crucial to the required performance of the plant. The MLSS concentration may be changed by altering the amount of sludge which is returned from the final sedimentation tank.

Sludge volume index (SVI)

This is measured to gauge the settleability of the sludge. As mentioned in Section 5.9.2, an SVI below 100 ml g^{-1} indicates a good settling sludge, whereas a result in excess of 180 ml g^{-1} would suggest that further investigation is needed.

Suspended solids content in the return sludge

This needs to be known in order to estimate how much sludge has to be recycled to maintain a given (F/M) ratio in the aeration tank. All the suspended solids are assumed to be composed of microbial mass which would add to the MLSS level in the aeration tank.

Microscopic examination

Microscopic examination by an experienced eye is an excellent method of judging the condition of an activated sludge system. Examination of the activated sludge for floc size and diversity of organisms can give an indication of the performance in the aeration tank. Filamentous organisms are undesirable. The presence of protozoa in the final effluent indicates a clear effluent.

SAQ 27

Compare the activated sludge process with the biological filter in terms of the merits and demerits of each.

See answer

5.9.11 Variants of the biological treatment system — *not examined*

Although activated sludge units and biological filters are probably the most common forms of biotreatment used in effluent treatment, variations do exist. Each of these variations has distinct advantages in treating a particular waste water and/or for a particular situation. A few examples of processes currently in use are given below.

Contact stabilisation

The contact stabilisation process takes advantage of the adsorptive properties of activated sludge. It has been postulated that BOD removal in the activated sludge process occurs in two phases. The first is the adsorptive phase taking some 20–40 minutes, in which soluble and colloidal, finely suspended organic matter is adsorbed by the activated sludge. In the second phase the adsorbed organics are assimilated metabolically. In the conventional activated sludge process, the two phases occur in the same tank. In contact stabilisation the two reactions take place in separate tanks. In this process (Figure 42) screened, degritted, settled effluent is mixed with return sludge and aerated in a contact tank for about 60 minutes. The sludge is then separated and aerated in a separate sludge stabilisation tank for 3–6 hours, where oxidation of the adsorbed material occurs. At the end of the aeration period the sludge is devoid of 'food' and thus readily adsorbs organic pollutants when put into the contact tank with fresh effluent. By concentrating the sludge before oxidation, total aeration tank volumes are

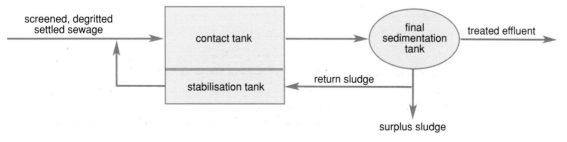

Figure 42 *The contact stabilisation process.*

reduced by approximately 50% compared with the conventional process. The contact stabilisation process is particularly suitable for waste waters in which a high proportion of the BOD is in suspended or colloidal form.

Oxidation ditch

In this system, biological oxidation takes place in a continuous 'race track'-shaped channel (Figure 43) in which the mixed liquor is circulated and aerated by brush aerators, which maintain a liquid velocity sufficient to prevent the settlement of sludge. The ditches are normally constructed in concrete and have a water depth of 1–2 m. They are trapezoidal in cross-section to maintain a uniform horizontal velocity throughout the depth of liquid. Large plants generally have channels of rectangular section and water depths of 3–4 m. Retention time in the ditch is in excess of 24 hours (extended aeration). The sludge age in oxidation ditches is normally 20–30 days. Consequently, the sludge solids undergo a considerable degree of stabilisation and aerobic digestion; the surplus sludge yield is said to be about 50% of the combined primary and secondary sludge from conventional activated sludge systems.

Nitrification usually takes place, owing to the long retention time and high sludge age provided, and the presence of an adequate supply of oxygen. Because there are time intervals between the passage of mixed liquor through successive aeration zones, denitrification can also occur, and in a number of cases the period allowed for passage through an anoxic zone (a zone devoid of oxygen) is deliberately increased (e.g. by switching off an aerator) to achieve a substantial reduction in the concentration of nitrate in the final effluent.

In the oxidation ditch system no primary sedimentation is required; thus screened, degritted effluent is fed straight into the ditch.

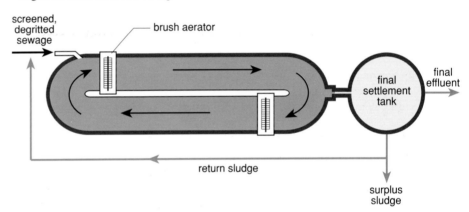

Figure 43   *The oxidation ditch system.*

The pure oxygen activated sludge process

Look at this definition in the set book.

It has been recognised that the use of pure oxygen rather than air in activated sludge systems can result in higher concentration driving forces and hence higher oxygen transfer rates per unit reactor volume. This allows a higher organic loading of the oxygen-fed reactor, compared with an air system. Thus an increase in plant capacity can be achieved without a corresponding increase in reactor volume. This feature would be attractive where severe space limitations are present. The oxygen required in the treatment process can be purchased as liquid oxygen or produced by on-site generation. In the latter, pressure swing adsorption is often utilised to adsorb nitrogen from air onto a molecular sieve, to give 80% oxygen-enriched air as a product. Typically, for a conventional air system the design organic loading would be 0.2–0.6 kg BOD kg^{-1} MLVSS d^{-1}, while for an oxygen it would be 0.4–1.0 kg BOD kg^{-1} MLVSS d^{-1}. An added advantage with pure oxygen systems is that the high dissolved oxygen levels enable nitrification to take place.

A commonly used pure oxygen activated sludge is the UNOX™ process developed by the Union Carbide Corporation. This system (Figure 44) consists of a series of completely mixed, roofed tanks, with the waste water and oxygen gas moving concurrently through them. In each stage mechanical aerators are used to distribute the oxygen throughout the waste water. The exhaust gases (containing carbon dioxide which inhibits bacterial action and which can also acidify the waste water) are withdrawn from the headspace.

The pure oxygen process has been shown to be particularly applicable where:

1   the available space for the construction of the treatment facilities is limited;

2   wide fluctuations occur in the organic loading to the plant;

3   strong waste waters are to be treated.

Care must be taken in pure oxygen systems to prevent explosive atmospheres arising from the possible discharge of hydrocarbons to the treatment plant. Materials of construction have to be carefully selected as corrosion proceeds more rapidly in an oxygen-rich environment.

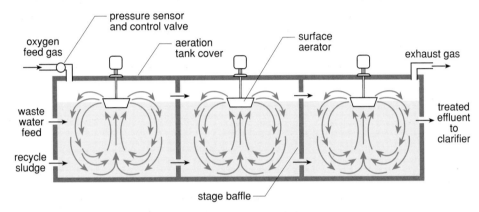

Figure 44   *The UNOX™ pure oxygen activated sludge process.*

The Deep Shaft ™ process

Look at *sewage treatment, deepshaft process* in the set book.

The Deep Shaft™ process is a form of high-intensity activated sludge treatment carried out in an underground shaft. The process was a spin-off from research into the production of protein from methanol, carried out by ICI in the 1970s. In the Deep Shaft process, raw sewage or strong biodegradable effluent, together with activated sludge, enters a vertical shaft (40–100 m deep; 0.5–10.0 m diameter) made of steel or concrete, where biodegradation takes place. No screening, grit settlement or primary sedimentation is required before the effluent enters the shaft. Solids are kept in suspension at the high flow velocity within the shaft and are carried out with the outflow. Allowing the solids to go through with the effluent results in a portion of them being degraded. The remaining materials (e.g. cloth, wood) are trapped by a screen downstream of the shaft. Grit settles out in the settling tank together with biomass. The shaft consists of an upflow section (the 'riser') and a downflow section (the 'downcomer') which may be concentric or side by side (Figure 45). To start circulation of the mixed liquor, compressed air is injected into the riser, reducing the density of the liquor and acting as an airlift. Since the header tank provides a common water level above both the riser and the downcomer, circulation begins. The supply of compressed air to the riser is then gradually reduced and transferred to the downcomer and, because the downward velocity of the liquid is greater than the upward velocity of the air bubbles, the entrained air is forced downwards. The air is rapidly dissolved in the water in the high pressure in the depths of the shaft and is readily available for use by the microorganisms. As the mixture travels up the riser and the pressure falls, bubbles of residual dissolved gases come out of solution, serving as an airlift, sustaining the circulation velocity of about 1.5 m s^{-1}. The effluent retention time

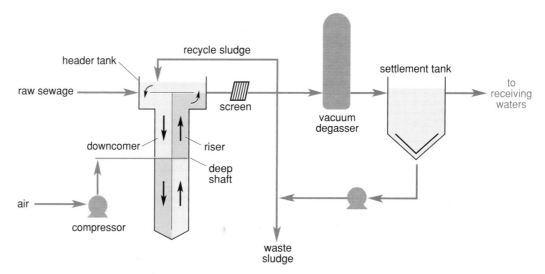

Figure 45   *The Deep Shaft™ process for treating domestic sewage.*

is 1–2 hours. The outflow of treated effluent from the shaft contains bubbles of nitrogen and carbon dioxide attached to the sludge flocs which hinder their settlement. The liquid is therefore degassed by passage through the header tank, and is usually assisted by a vacuum device or by coarse-bubble stripping. The mixed liquor, now free from entrained gases, passes forward to the settlement tank, where sludge settles, to be recycled or taken away for disposal.

In the treatment of sewage in the Deep Shaft process, oxygen utilisation may be as high as 90% (compared with 20% in the conventional activated sludge system) and the oxygen uptake intensity as high as 1 kg O_2 m^{-3} h^{-1} at peak flow (compared with <0.2 kg O_2 m^{-3} h^{-1} in the conventional activated sludge process). This high oxygen uptake results from the greater dissolution of the oxygen at the high pressure in the shaft and the long bubble contact time (about 90 seconds, compared with about 15 seconds in conventional diffused air systems). This results in lower power consumption and a lower aeration volume requirement. It has been observed that in the Deep Shaft process the amount of sludge generated is less than in the conventional system, due to the complex microbiological reactions occurring in the shaft. This has a positive effect on the operating costs of the treatment process, since sludge disposal is a major cost item in wastewater treatment. Another major advantage of the Deep Shaft process is that it requires much less land area than a conventional system treating the same load. For this reason it has found acceptance in densely populated cities where land availability is at a premium.

The rotating biological contactor

The rotating biological contactor (RBC) (Figure 46) is a system which combines the advantages of both the activated sludge system (long retention time in the active area, small space needed for plant) and the biological filter (sludge return not necessary, easy to operate and needing little maintenance or supervision). It has been employed as a sewage treatment plant for small communities. The sewage influent, after passing through a primary settlement tank, goes into a tank in which an assembly of vertical discs (usually made of glass reinforced plastic) is slowly rotated by an electric motor at a speed of about three revolutions per minute. Usually about 40% of the area of these discs is submerged. The discs serve as physical support surfaces for the growth of microorganisms and the rotation provides alternate immersion and aeration of the organisms. The discs are fluted or otherwise designed to increase the surface area available for the biological film to grow on.

The RBC is similar to a biological filter in that both rely on microbes attached to a surface for biotreatment, but the RBC is more compact and does not result in a fly problem – because the biological film is immersed periodically in the sewage, flies do not colonise the discs. RBCs either have covers or are housed in buildings.

Figure 46 *A rotating biological contactor with cover removed.*

RBCs are quiet, require little attention, and can be made unobtrusive by being positioned partly below ground level. These factors make them suitable for small groups of houses or for caravan and camp sites. The RBC has been restricted to relatively small installations due to its high construction cost relative to an activated sludge system.

Waste stabilisation ponds

Waste stabilisation ponds are a simple means of treating waste water biologically by harnessing the power of sunlight and wind. In this type of system, screened, degritted effluent is passed through a series of ponds with a total retention time of 10–50 days. In the ponds, bacteria oxidise the pollutants and work symbiotically with algae which provide oxygen through photosynthesis. The algae also utilise the carbon dioxide, ammonia and phosphate that are released by the bacteria. Aeration also occurs through the action of wind. No mechanical equipment is used in the ponds and hence operation and maintenance costs are very low. A typical layout for a waste stabilisation pond system treating domestic sewage is shown in Figure 47.

The major part of the biodegradation of the sewage takes place in the *facultative* ponds (1–1.5 m deep), which are aerobic at the top and anaerobic at the bottom. *Maturation* ponds are usually about 1 m deep and serve to inactivate pathogenic bacteria and viruses through the action of UV radiation from sunlight, the high pH of the water due to algal activity, and the high dissolved oxygen content generated by the greater algal activity in these shallow ponds. The long retention time in each of the ponds also enhances the sedimentation of parasite eggs and dormant forms of some parasitic organisms. In instances where the waste water is of very high BOD (e.g. effluent from the intensive rearing of animals), *anaerobic* ponds are often used ahead of the facultative ponds. Anaerobic ponds are 2–4 m deep and are nearly totally devoid of oxygen.

Waste stabilisation ponds are especially efficient in hot climates but are also used in colder areas: for example, in France there are about 2000 waste stabilisation pond systems, in Germany there are about 1000, and in the USA about one-third of all wastewater treatment plants are of this type. Most of the systems in France and Germany serve populations of less than 1000. Though they require large areas of land, this need can be satisfied by locating the ponds at the outer perimeter of cities, or on disused land.

Treated sewage can be reused in irrigation if safe limits of faecal coliforms and intestinal nematode eggs are achieved in the treatment process. Table 8 gives the relevant

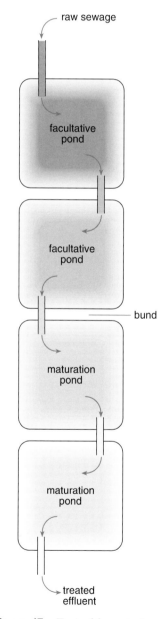

Figure 47 *Typical layout of a waste stabilisation pond system treating domestic sewage.*

Table 8 *Recommended microbiological quality guidelines[a] for wastewater use in agriculture*

Category	Reuse conditions	Exposed group	Intestinal Nematodes[b] (arithmetic mean no. of eggs per litre)	Faecal coliforms (geometric mean no. per 100 ml[c])	Wastewater treatment expected to achieve the required microbiological quality
A	Irrigation of crops likely to be eaten uncooked, sports fields, public parks	Workers, consumers, public	<1	<1000[d]	A series of stabilisation ponds designed to achieve the microbiological quality indicated, or equivalent treatment.
B	Irrigation of cereal crops, industrial crops, pasture and trees[e]	Workers	<1	No standard requirement	Retention in stabilisation ponds for 8–10 days or equivalent helminth and faecal coliform removal.
C	Localised irrigation of crops in Category B if exposure of workers and the public does not occur	None	Not applicable	Not applicable	Pretreatment as required by the irrigation technology, but not less than primary sedimentation.

[a]In specific cases, local epidemiological, sociocultural and environmental factors should be taken into account and the guidelines modified accordingly.

[b]*Ascaris* and *Trichuris* species and hookworms.

[c]During the irrigation period.

[d]A more stringent guideline (<200 faecal coliforms per 100 ml) is appropriate for public lawns, such as hotel lawns, with which the public may come into direct contact.

[e]In the case of fruit trees, irrigation should cease two weeks before fruit is picked and no fruit should be picked off the ground. Sprinkler irrigation should not be used.

Source: World Health Organization (1989) 'Health guidelines for the use of wastewater in agriculture and aquaculture', WHO Technical Report Series **778**, WHO, Geneva.

World Health Organisation guidelines. Waste stabilisation ponds have been found capable of attaining these standards at low cost and are actively encouraged as a means of supplementing the water supply available for irrigation, especially in developing countries and in southern Europe, e.g. in Portugal. At the same time as treating waste water, pond systems have been used to increase protein production through the rearing of fish and ducks in maturation ponds.

Reed beds

Species of the common reed *Phragmites* have been used to treat domestic and industrial waste waters in Europe. In a well-prepared reed bed (Figure 48) the reeds are planted in rows in a pit which has been first sealed at the bottom with clay and/or a synthetic liner, and then had soil placed on top of it.

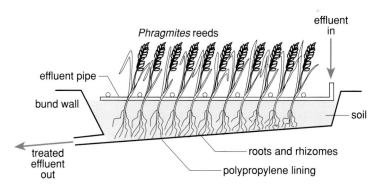

Figure 48 *The reed bed system.*

The effluent to be treated is distributed through pipes and nozzles onto the reed bed. The effluent percolates through the soil to the roots and rhizomes of the reeds, where the resident microorganisms degrade the organic components of the waste water. The oxygen required by the microorganisms is obtained through the leaves of the *Phragmites* and from the air. Oxygen is taken in through the stomata (apertures) in the underside of the leaves and passed down the hollow stem of the plant to the underground rhizome and root system. The pollutants are converted to carbon dioxide, nitrogen and water, with little sludge being produced. Some anaerobic degradation will also take place.

Owing to the great diversity of microbial species in the soil, greater potential treatment is possible: for example, the fungal species *Actinomyces*, *Streptomyces* and *Basidiomyces*, which are capable of biodegrading many synthetic chemicals such as the common pesticides and chlorinated hydrocarbons, are found in soil but are not normally in effluent treatment plants.

Reed beds are used to treat screened, degritted sewage in several countries in Europe (e.g. in Denmark and Germany). A few systems exist in the UK. A major chemical manufacturer in Billingham, England, is using reed beds to treat industrial effluent containing traces of phenol, methanol, acetone and amines. It is claimed that reed beds have also been used to remove toxic organics and heavy metals from leachates from landfill sites.

At maturity the reeds are 1.5–3.0 m high. Unlike mechanical treatment plants they are not unsightly or noisy. They are almost as expensive as mechanical treatment plants to set up but their running costs are low and they have no sludge disposal costs.

The main disadvantage with reed beds is the amount of land they require. In order to give the desired level of treatment to chemical wastes which are difficult to dispose of, the reeds may require several years to grow to full maturity.

Septic tanks

Septic tanks are often used for the disposal of sewage in areas which, for practical reasons, are not sewered (for instance, the effluent flow generated in the area may be small and intermittent, such as in farms or individual residences dispersed in the

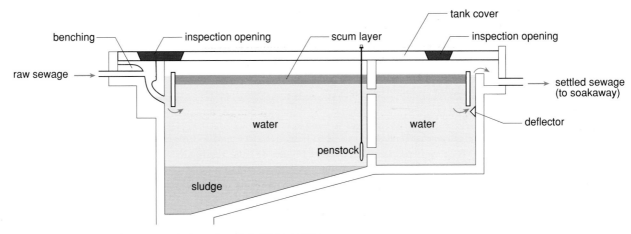

Figure 49   *A typical septic tank (based on BS 6297: 1983).*

countryside). Septic tanks usually have two compartments (Figure 49) and are buried underground. The first compartment (which is usually twice the size of the second) provides for sedimentation, sludge digestion and sludge storage. The second compartment provides additional sedimentation and sludge-storage capacity and thus serves to protect against the discharge of sludge and other material that might escape the first chamber. A thick crust of scum usually forms at the water surface of the tank. The organic solids that sediment out are partially digested by anaerobic bacteria. Sludge accumulates and the tank must be desludged occasionally, typically every 12 months, depending on loading. The sludge is tankered to a wastewater treatment plant for treatment and disposal. Experience has shown that in order to provide sufficiently quiescent conditions for effective sedimentation of the sewage solids in septic tanks, the liquid retention time should be at least 24 hours. Two-thirds of the tank volume is usually reserved for the storage of accumulated sludge and scum, so the size of the septic tank should be based on a 3-day retention time at start-up.

Effluent from a septic tank usually flows into a soakaway (a chamber with perforated or open-jointed walls) from where it percolates into the ground. In selecting a site for a soakaway it is important to consider the ability of the ground to absorb water, its permeability and the varying level of the water table with the seasons of the year.

5.9.12   Package treatment plants

The sewage from small groups of houses in remote locations is often treated in package treatment plants. These are compact, complete treatment systems which are prefabricated and hence easily installed. They are relatively simple to operate. They have all the unit operations of a full-scale sewage treatment plant except that they are smaller in size (to treat the low flows present).

Both activated sludge and biological filters can be made as package units. Being small in size, package treatment plants are able to use non-concrete tanks, e.g. tanks made of glass-reinforced plastic. This also makes them easy to transport. Rotating biological contactors are particularly favoured for package plants as they can be built partially below ground level and therefore do not significantly visually impair the landscape.

5.9.13   Chemical treatment of sewage

The various biological processes of sewage treatment could be replaced by chemical processes, such as coagulation and flocculation.

Advantages of chemical methods include their ability to process sewage at a faster rate, and they are also unaffected by toxic substances and changes in loading and temperature, whereas the organisms responsible for the effectiveness of biological processes are very susceptible to such factors.

The two main disadvantages are cost and the volume of sludge produced. Chemical reagents are very expensive – oxidising bacteria can be exploited for approximately

5% of the cost of the cheapest chemical oxidising agent. Chemical methods, operating by precipitation, produce large volumes of sludge that contain both the solids removed from the sewage and most of the added chemicals. In biological treatment, the quantity of sludge produced is less because bacterial oxidation also results in the formation of carbon dioxide from organic carbon.

In the final analysis, however, it is economics that dictates the treatment process to be adopted. For biodegradable pollutants, biodegradation works out as the more favourable of the two.

5.9.14 Waterless sewage treatment

Water-borne disposal of sewage uses up vast quantities of water. Using the traditional lavatory flush system, each person utilises some 45 litres every day of *clean, potable water* to transport 135–270 g of solid waste and 1.0–1.3 l of liquid waste to the sewage treatment plant. The sewers and treatment plants needed to handle the tremendous volumes of waste water generated by communities of people are costly, both in capital and in operation and maintenance. It would be much more prudent for sewage to be disposed of at source (i.e. within the compound of the house, factory, etc. where it is generated) using dry methods such as *composting*. Then sewers and treatment plants need only handle sullage (and rainwater run-off) and can be smaller in size and cost. The composting of the sewage could take place with other biodegradable domestic wastes, such as food waste. The composted material (free of pathogenic organisms – see Units 8–10) can be used beneficially in agriculture or horticulture, thus recycling valuable nutrients. Well-designed, dry composting toilets are being marketed at the present time.

If there is an opportunity for on-site reuse of waste water, it may be feasible to treat the sullage at source, and reuse it too. Treatment by sedimentation (removal of solids), skimming (removal of oil and fat) and disinfection (to eliminate pathogens) may be adequate for many secondary uses such as irrigation.

If we are to conserve water and recycle nutrients usefully, the path to follow is perhaps the increased adoption of waterless sanitary disposal systems. The obstacle to be overcome, however, is the perceived nature of sewage by the public. The idea that sewage is an obnoxious waste has to be replaced by the view that it is a valuable resource.

SAQ 28

Consider the different types of effluents given in Column A and select from Column B the most appropriate treatment technique for each of the effluents.

Column A	Column B
A Domestic sewage from a single cottage in the countryside	Pure oxygen activated sludge process
B An effluent with a high concentration of colloidal particles	Reed beds
C Domestic and farm waste waters in a sparsely populated rural area with a lot of land available	Rotating biological contactor
D A high-BOD effluent from a food processing plant in a built-up area with little available land	Oxidation ditch
E Domestic effluent from a remote group of houses in an area of low soil permeability	Contact stabilisation
F An effluent with a high ammonia content from a fertiliser plant which has extensive land available	Septic tank
G An industrial effluent with traces of mixed organics not easily degraded in a conventional mechanical plant	Deep Shaft process
H A mixed industrial–sanitary waste water with a high and fluctuating organic load, in a city site	Waste stabilisation ponds

not examined

5.10   Tertiary treatment

The processes so far described can produce an effluent containing no more than 30 g m^{-3} of suspended solids and 20 g m^{-3} of BOD, but sometimes more stringent standards may be necessary as, for example, when the effluent forms such a substantial part of a river flow that a dilution of less than 8:1 results, or when the river is used for a public water supply. In such cases the effluent should not contain suspended solids greater in concentration than 10 g m^{-3}, or have a BOD greater than 10 g m^{-3}, or contain ammonia-nitrogen in excess of 10 g m^{-3}. This standard is often referred to as the 10/10 standard (strictly speaking, the 10/10/10 standard). The additional processes beyond secondary treatment required to reach such a standard comprise tertiary treatment.

5.10.1   Suspended solids removal

Systems typically used to remove suspended solids in tertiary treatment are described below. The reduction in suspended solids also results in a lowering of the BOD because some of the solids are organic matter which contributes to the BOD.

Microstraining

The microstrainers (see Section 4.2) used in sewage treatment retain solids with diameters larger than about 45 μm. The trapped solids are returned to the inlet of the treatment works. To reduce costs, the final effluent is often used as the wash water. To prevent biological growth on the fabric of the microstrainer (as a result of nutrients present in the treated effluent), a UV light is usually mounted alongside the wash-water jets.

Sand filtration

The effluent from biological treatment is passed through rapid gravity sand filters, and the solid matter which has been trapped in the bed is removed by backwashing. The washings are pumped back to the inlet of the works.

Further settlement

Settlement of the final effluent will improve its overall quality. This may be carried out in special settlement lagoons similar to maturation ponds (see 'Waste stabilisation ponds' in Section 5.9.11). During storage in the lagoons, the quality of the water improves as a result of some of the solids settling and the activity of bacteria, protozoa and algae. Suspended solids, BOD, pathogenic bacteria, nitrate and phosphate can all be reduced. The construction of such lagoons will take up a considerable area of land and add to the total costs of the treatment works. This cost can be avoided if storm tanks are used instead. The procedure would be always to have one storm tank empty. During storm conditions this empty tank would be filled first. While it is filling, the other storm tanks would be emptied to allow them to receive the storm water. Once the storm is over the tanks can then be emptied and returned to their tertiary treatment function.

> The use of extended settlement seems simple and not overcostly. Can you think of any drawbacks in the process?

In a water with a good supply of oxygen, nitrate and phosphate, there is a strong possibility of algal growth and this could result in the effluent having a higher suspended solids content than the influent to the tertiary treatment process. But the presence of algae in the discharge is not altogether undesirable. The algae, if able to continue photosynthesising, can contribute to the oxygenation of the receiving water. The algae could also increase the productivity of the receiving water. (For instance, algae would be 'food' to shellfish in coastal waters). Finally, the non-toxic algae from the tertiary treatment process may be able to multiply and out-compete toxic algal species such as the blue-greens present in the receiving waterway. As an aside, lagoons can also develop into attractive semi-natural habitats that can be valuable for wildlife.

Grass plots

In this method the treated effluent is allowed to trickle slowly over grassland. The use of grass plots will result in a further reduction of the BOD and solids, but it has the disadvantage of requiring large areas of land with the correct characteristics, e.g. a slope of not greater than 1 in 60. Each cubic metre of effluent flow per day requires an area of 1.2 m^2 of grassland.

Reed beds can also be used to improve the quality of a 30/20 effluent. Lagoon, grass plot and reed bed treatment also remove the nutrients nitrate and phosphate, and so reduce the possibility of eutrophication in the receiving watercourse.

Specific processes for N, P and ammonia removal can also be considered to be tertiary treatment operations.

5.10.2 Nitrate removal

Nitrates remaining in the effluent after secondary treatment can be removed using fluidised bed reactors, described in Section 4.8.1.

Reverse osmosis and electrodialysis with nitrate-selective membranes are currently being evaluated as possible cost-effective alternatives.

5.10.3 Phosphorus removal

Phosphorus may be present in waste water as orthophosphate, polyphosphate, and as organic phosphorus. Typically its concentration in domestic waste water is 8 mg l^{-1} and it originates from human body wastes (primarily urine), food wastes, and from household detergents and cleaning compounds. About 10% of the phosphorus in domestic waste water is insoluble and is removed in primary sedimentation. Some of the remainder (soluble) phosphorus is incorporated into new bacterial cells in biological oxidation but the major part remains in solution. In the biological oxidation stage of treatment most of the organic phosphorus and the polyphosphates are converted to orthophosphate. Phosphorus in the orthophosphate form is easily precipitated using chemicals such as lime, alum, ferric chloride or ferric sulphate. The residual organic phosphorus and polyphosphates are removed by adsorption on to the precipitate.

The reactions of orthophosphate with lime, alum and ferric chloride are:

lime $\quad\quad\quad 5Ca^{2+} + 3PO_4^{3-} + OH^- \rightleftharpoons Ca_5(PO_4)_3OH$ (hydroxyapatite)

alum $\quad\quad\quad Al_2(SO_4)_3 \cdot 14H_2O + 2PO_4^{3-} \rightleftharpoons 2AlPO_4 + 3SO_4^{2-} + 14H_2O$

iron (III) chloride $FeCl_3 + PO_4^{3-} \rightleftharpoons FePO_4 + 3Cl^-$

Phosphate removal of 30–40% is claimed to be possible through the use of reed beds. In activated sludge systems, phosphate removal can be enhanced by applying a sequence of anaerobic and aerobic conditions which induce polyphosphate storage in microorganisms.

5.10.4 Ammonia removal

Domestic sewage typically contains 25 mg l^{-1} of ammoniacal nitrogen. If high ammonia waste waters are treated, a high residual quantity may be present in the secondary-treated effluent. Ammonia in the discharged effluent is undesirable for several reasons:

- it creates an oxygen demand;
- it contributes to algal blooms;
- in the free form it is toxic to fish and other aquatic animals;
- if present in water used as a source of potable supply, it combines with chlorine in the disinfection stage, reducing its effectiveness as a disinfectant and increasing the chlorine demand of the water;

- it accelerates corrosion of structures (e.g. bridges, water intake systems) in the water;

- it can be converted to nitrates, which would have other problems.

Ammonia nitrogen exists in aqueous solution as either the ammonium ion (NH_4^+) or free ammonia (NH_3), depending on the pH of the solution, in accordance with the following equilibrium reaction:

$$NH_3 + H_2O \rightleftharpoons NH_4^+ + OH^-$$

At pH levels above 7, the equilibrium is displaced to the left and free ammonia predominates; at pH levels below 7 the equilibrium is shifted to the right and the ammonium ion predominates.

Ammonia can be removed from waste water in several ways. The methods commonly used are described below.

Biological nitrification/denitrification

In this method, probably the most economical means of removing ammonia, microorganisms are used (usually in an attached growth system) to convert the ammonia to nitrite and then to nitrate:

$$2NH_4^+ + 3O_2 \qquad\qquad 2NO_2^- + 2H_2O + 4H^+$$
$$2NO_2^- + O_2 \qquad\qquad 2NO_3^-$$

This is exactly the same process, referred to in Section 5.9.1, that normally will take place in biological filters during secondary treatment. It also occurs in soil and natural waters (see also Unit 2). The nitrates formed are then converted to nitrogen gas in an anoxic reactor because the denitrifying bacteria are anaerobic. A carbon source (typically methanol, CH_3OH) is added to facilitate the conversion:

$$6NO_3^- + 2CH_3OH \rightarrow 6NO_2^- + 2CO_2 + 4H_2O$$
$$6NO_2^- + 3CH_3OH \rightarrow 3N_2 + 3CO_2 + 3H_2O + 6OH^-$$

Common denitrifying bacteria are *Pseudomonas denitrificans* and the *Hyphomicrobium* species.

Air stripping

As mentioned above, at pH values above 7 ammonium ions are converted to free ammonia. In air stripping, the waste water pH is increased using lime to about 11.0 (when 98% of the ammonia content is in the free form, i.e. NH_3 gas) and the waste water then passed through a packed tower in which air is blown countercurrently (Figure 50). The ammonia gas is stripped out of solution by the air.

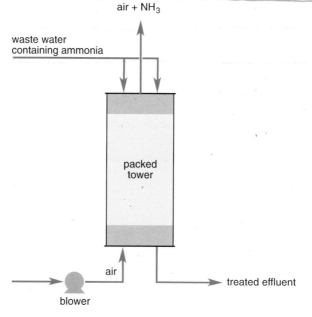

Figure 50   *Diagram of a stripping column to remove ammonia from waste water.*

Breakpoint chlorination

In this method, chlorine, which is an oxidising agent, is used in excess to oxidise the ammonia-nitrogen in solution to nitrogen gas, according to the equations:

$$2NH_3 + 2HOCl \rightarrow 2NH_2Cl + 2H_2O$$
$$2NH_2Cl + HOCl \rightarrow N_2 + H_2O + 3HCl$$

Overall reaction: $2NH_3 + 3HOCl \rightarrow N_2 + 3H_2O + 3HCl$

The optimum pH operating range for breakpoint chlorination has been found to be 6–7. Outside this range, the chlorine dosage required to reach the breakpoint increases significantly and the rate of reaction slows. The chlorine dose required for breakpoint chlorination is about ten times the concentration of ammonia present and is thus economically prohibitive except for special situations and where the ammonia concentration has already been significantly reduced.

Ion exchange

Clinoptilolite, a natural rock, has been found to be very effective in removing ammonia from waste water. It can be regenerated using a solution of lime. The ammonium ions removed from the clinoptilolite are converted to ammonia because of the high pH. The ammonia is removed by passing the regeneration solution through a stripping tower (see above). The stripped liquid is then collected for subsequent reuse.

5.11 Advanced wastewater treatment

Even after tertiary treatment an effluent could still contain impurities which might cause problems in the receiving water or interfere with a future use of the receiving water. The methods used to remove these impurities are usually classified under advanced wastewater treatment (AWT).

Some of the typical AWT processes are:

1   *Adsorption using activated carbon*. Adsorption on activated carbon may be used for the removal of residual non-biodegradable organic substances such as pesticides, or for the removal of compounds causing colour, taste and odour.

2   *Reverse osmosis*. Reverse osmosis can be used to remove all the suspended solids present in tertiary-treated water. The process also removes any high molecular weight solutes present.

3   *Disinfection*. In many countries the reuse of treated sewage for irrigation of trees and bushes, fodder crops, and crops that have to be cooked prior to eating (e.g. potatoes, onions) is encouraged. Disinfection of the treated effluent is carried out to render it free of pathogens. Typically, tertiary-treated effluent of 10/10 standard is treated with chlorine. The chlorine added will initially be consumed by any ammonia present, and then a free residual will develop. In instances where treated sewage is discharged into the sea, disinfection is often carried out to prevent pathogens reaching bathing areas. Cross-flow microfilters are being tested for the removal of bacteria and viruses, and disinfection by UV and by peracetic acid is being evaluated. (A molecule of peracetic acid or peroxyacetic consists of a molecule of acetic acid with an additional oxygen atom.) Cross-flow microfiltration would remove the pathogens by a purely physical process. In order to protect the environment from potentially harmful compounds produced as by-products of chemical disinfection, the National Rivers Authority prefers non-chemical methods of eliminating pathogens. These would include microfiltration and UV radiation.

Disinfection of treated sewage to protect bathing areas is a short-term measure. In the long term, the outfall pipes will have to be lengthened or relocated to eliminate the possibility of the effluent reaching bathing waters.

SAQ 29

When is tertiary treatment likely to be required for the final effluent from a sewage works?

If the effluent from a sewage works has to be improved but there is little space for construction at the works, which of the tertiary treatment processes could be selected?

SAQ 30

Which of the following statements about sewage effluent would be applicable after its treatment?

A   It will contain at most 30 g m^{-3} of suspended solids and have a BOD of 20 g m^{-3}.
B   It will conform to standards depending on the needs of the watercourse receiving it.
C   It will not be a risk to public health.
D   It will be potable.
E   It will not contain any polluting substances.
F   It will not contain any suspended solids or toxic chemicals or have a BOD.

TMA Q1   See answer (handwritten note; B circled)

SAQ 31

Complete the following diagram on sewage treatment.

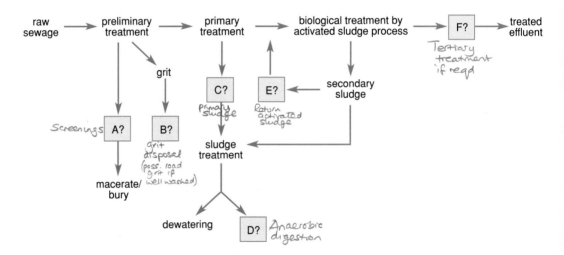

5.12   Summary

The aims of sewage treatment are to reduce the content of biodegradable material in the sewage, and to eliminate any toxic materials and pathogenic organisms present in the effluent.

Sewage treatment by the traditional mechanical/biological method can include some or all of the following processes: screening, grit removal, comminution, primary sedimentation, biological oxidation and secondary sedimentation. In biological oxidation, bacteria convert the soluble and colloidal organic matter into new cell material. This cell material is removed as sludge in the secondary sedimentation tank. The effluent after biological treatment and sedimentation should be of 30/20 quality or better, i.e. with suspended solids content not exceeding 30 g m^{-3} and BOD not exceeding 20 g m^{-3}.

Activated sludge units and biological filters are the main types of bioreactor in wastewater treatment. Many variants of the two exist, each with advantages for a particular waste water or situation. The greatest potential for cost-effective treatment and safe reuse of sewage lies in waterless sanitary disposal systems but these have first to gain public acceptance.

Tertiary treatment may be carried out when a particularly high quality effluent is required. The suspended solids (and associated BOD) concentration is reduced using processes such as microstraining, sand filtration, settlement, and grass plots. Elimination of nitrates may be effected using fluidised bed reactors. Phosphorus removal is possible by precipitation using lime, alum, ferric chloride or ferric sulphate. Ammonia may be removed by biological nitrification/denitrification, air stripping, breakpoint chlorination, or ion exchange.

Further purification of the treated effluent is possible using advanced water treatment techniques such as activated carbon adsorption, reverse osmosis and disinfection.

6   SLUDGE TREATMENT AND DISPOSAL

6.1   Introduction

Sludge is the inevitable product of removing solids from, and reducing the BOD of, sewage and trade (industrial) wastes. While the liquid part of sewage can be treated satisfactorily, the treatment and disposal of sludge presents the greatest problems for pollution control. Unsatisfactory methods of disposal can lead to further pollution. Sludge treatment and disposal may represent up to 50% of the total cost of sewage treatment.

6.2   Sludge production and sludge characteristics

Sewage sludge is a direct result of the presence of solids in suspension and an indirect result of the biological treatment of dissolved and emulsified organic matter. The volume of sludge generated in sewage treatment is 1–2% of the volume of sewage treated.

The sludge separated during the treatment processes is an evil-smelling, highly putrescible, thick liquid containing a considerable quantity of water. Table 9 indicates how much sludge may be expected from each treatment process per head of population.

Table 9   *Quantity and water content of sludge generated in different operations in wastewater treatment*

Source of sludge	Quantity/ (kg per head per day)	Water content/% (wet basis)
Primary sedimentation	1.1	95.5
Biological filters		
(a) Low-rate filters	0.23	93.9
(b) High-rate filters	0.30	94.0
Activated sludge unit	2.4	98.5

Exercise

How many kilograms of dry solid matter are produced per head per day from primary sedimentation sludge?

Answer

From Table 9, primary sedimentation sludge has a water content of 95.5%, i.e. for every 1 kg of sludge, 0.955 kg is water. So out of 1.1 kg of sludge per head per day, the quantity of dry solid matter is given by

$$(1 - 0.955)(1.1) = 0.0495 \text{ kg}$$

Exercise

What volume of sludge is produced per day from an activated sludge process in a sewage treatment works serving a town of 20 000 population? Take the sludge density as 1200 kg m^{-3}.

Answer

For a town of 20 000 the total quantity of surplus sludge from the activated sludge process is

$$(20\,000)(2.4) = 48\,000 \text{ kg d}^{-1}$$

This is equivalent to a volume of

$$\frac{48\,000}{1200} = 40 \text{ m}^3 \text{ d}^{-1}$$

In addition to sludge as a by-product of primary and secondary treatment, 0.02–0.2 m^3 of grit are found in every thousand cubic metres of sewage. Note the comparatively high water content or low percentage of solid matter contained in activated sludge. This is a result of the complicated nature of activated sludge and the interaction of the forces between its particles. The organic component of sewage sludge consists of grease and fats, proteins and cellulose which are produced by the human population as a result of their eating habits.

The sludge produced in sewage treatment will have a wide range of constituents. A combined sewerage system collects solids from hard surface areas and this slightly affects the amount of sludge generated. A particular contribution comes from grit that is spread on roads during frosty weather. Although grit removal is incorporated early on in the system, not all the grit is removed and some inevitably passes on to appear in the sludge. Sludge contains 20–30% mineral matter, most of which is grit. The composition of sludge is also affected by the trade effluents discharged into the treatment works. There may be inorganic material from metal industry wastes, or organic matter from slaughterhouses and distilleries.

The amounts and characteristics of solid matter in trade effluents vary despite the limits that are placed on the suspended solids, BOD, metals, etc., when a consent is given to discharge wastes to a sewer. Sludge can also contain toxic material which has been removed from the sewage during treatment and it is this toxic material which restricts the use of sludge as a soil fertiliser or conditioner.

Before disposal the sludge will require treatment.

6.3   Methods of treatment

Table 9 showed that over 90% of sewage sludge is water; thus, before disposal can be considered, the sludge leaving the works should be dewatered to reduce the volume and weight of material for disposal. The dewatering also helps to prevent the sludge from decomposing and creating unpleasant odours. To improve the efficiency of dewatering it is often necessary to include a preliminary conditioning stage to release as much of the bound water as possible and to allow the solids to agglomerate. There are several such conditioning processes which can be used. The method chosen will depend on the characteristics of the sludge.

The sludge can be thickened by coagulation, flocculation and sedimentation. Chemicals such as aluminium sulphate, iron salts, lime and polyelectrolyte can be used as coagulants (see Section 4.3). Thickening takes place in a tank equipped with a low-moving paddle or set of tines. Sludge settles and supernatant is drawn off. The coagulants used are costly but the increase in solids content of the thickened sludge can make up for the extra cost involved.

After the preliminary conditioning, the sludge can be further treated to increase the solids content by mechanical dewatering.

The traditional method of dewatering sludge is by air-drying on open beds. These drying beds consist of large areas (0.5 m^2 per person served by the sewage treatment works) usually surfaced with sand or ash and enclosed by low walls. The beds are filled with wet sludge to a depth of approximately 0.2 m and left until the sludge (cake) is dry enough (20–50% solids content) to be removed by hand or by mechanical methods. This method of treatment is entirely dependent upon the weather. During the summer the sludge may be fit for removal after two weeks, but in the winter it may be months before the sludge can be removed. Drying beds often give rise to offensive smells. The main argument advanced for their continued use is that they require only a small labour force using automatic means (or a shovel) for lifting and conveying the sludge cake. They are usually only found on small rural works.

Other methods of dewatering use mechanical systems and include pressure filtration, vacuum filtration and centrifuging. These were detailed in Section 4.11. The extracted water, high in BOD and suspended solids, is directed to the treatment works inlet.

Anaerobic digestion can also be carried out. Here, thickened sludge in an airtight tank, usually at 35 °C, is converted to methane and carbon dioxide by anaerobic bacteria. Two types of digesters are used – standard rate and high rate digesters. In the standard rate digester (Figure 51a) the contents are usually not heated or mixed. The retention time of the sludge is 30–60 days. In the high-rate digester (Figure 51b) the contents are heated and completely mixed and the retention time is 15 days or less. A combination of the two is called a two-stage process (Figure 51c). In the second stage of this process, in addition to digestion and gas production, separation of the digested solids from the liquor takes place.

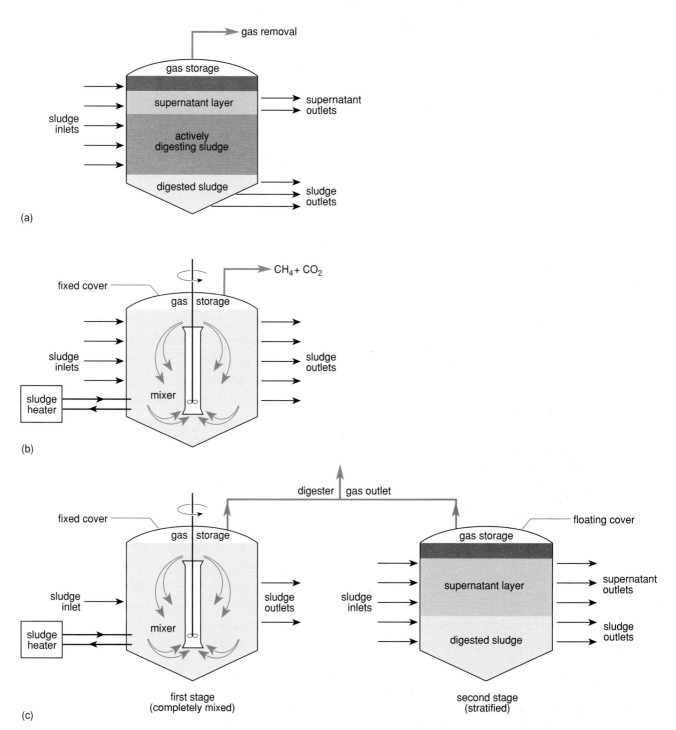

Figure 51   *Anaerobic digesters: (a) conventional, standard-rate, single stage process; (b) stirred tank, high-rate, single stage process; (c) two-stage process.*

The digestion process occurs in two steps:

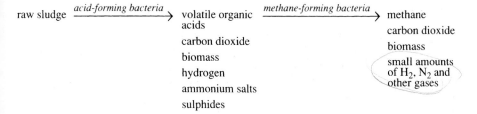

raw sludge $\xrightarrow{\textit{acid-forming bacteria}}$ volatile organic acids
carbon dioxide
biomass
hydrogen
ammonium salts
sulphides
$\xrightarrow{\textit{methane-forming bacteria}}$ methane
carbon dioxide
biomass
small amounts of H_2, N_2 and other gases

In the first step, acid-forming bacteria (such as *Clostridium* spp, *Desulphovibrio* spp) convert the complex organic material in the sludge to volatile organic acids (such as acetic, propionic and butyric acids) and other compounds. In the second step, methane-forming bacteria (e.g. *Methanobacterium*, and *Methanobacillus* spp) transform the volatile organic acids to methane and carbon dioxide. Many of the methane-forming organisms identified in anaerobic digesters are similar to those found in the stomachs of ruminant animals and in organic sediments taken from lakes and rivers.

The methane gas comes out of the digester with carbon dioxide in the proportions 65–70% CH_4 and 25–30% CO_2 and can be used as an energy source – it is usually used to heat the digester contents to maintain the temperature at 35 °C. Any surplus can be used to heat the offices and laboratories at the treatment plant. Small amounts of H_2, and N_2 and other gases may also emerge from the digester.

The pH of the digester should be controlled at about 7.0 since the rate of methane production slows down below this value. Adequate alkalinity (1000–5000 g m^{-3} as $CaCO_3$) is required to buffer the sludge. Toxic material input should be controlled, e.g. heavy metal concentration should not exceed 1 ppm.

Sludge can be introduced continuously or intermittently. The stabilised sludge has a total solids content 35–40% lower in volume compared with the input. It is not malodorous and is smoother and darker in comparison with the input sludge. Pathogenic organisms are much reduced in number.

In anaerobic digestion, organic nitrogen compounds are broken down to ammonia and ammonium salts giving much increased concentrations of nitrogen in the liquid phase. This increases the immediate availability of nitrogen to crops if the wet sludge is used as a manure and soil conditioner on agricultural land.

The supernatant from digesters is highly polluting and can be a problem. Normally it is returned to the works inlet for treatment. This is usually done at night when the incoming sewage flow is low and the plant is underloaded.

6.4   Methods of disposal

Sludge may be spread on land (land application), dumped in sludge lagoons, buried, composted with household refuse, dumped in landfill sites, dumped at sea, or incinerated. Of the total sewage sludge produced in the UK, about 65% is applied to agricultural land, 31% is dumped at sea, and the remaining 4% is incinerated.

Land application

The traditional method of disposal is to spread the sludge on agricultural land where it is beneficial as a soil conditioner. It is often ploughed in after it has dried further. Usually the sludge is disposed of in this way after storage for some months in open tanks, which reduces the risk of nuisance or transmission of disease. The risk is also reduced by ploughing the sludge in. This method requires large areas of land and suitable weather conditions.

The value of sludge as a fertiliser is not high. Typically, anaerobically digested sludge contains 5.0% nitrogen, 2% phosphate and 0.2% potash. This is insignificant compared with the nutrients applied each year as artificial fertilisers. However, the organic matter in sludge forms a humus which can be a useful soil conditioner. Most sludge is produced in large urban areas and it can be extremely expensive to transport it to farming areas where it is given free to farmers. A further practical difficulty is that farmers only require sludge at certain times of the year whereas it is produced all the year round. The amount of agricultural land able to take sludge is also limited.

Many urban sewage works process a significant amount of industrial waste in addition to household waste. As a result, toxic materials (e.g. toxic metals) concentrate in the sludge and restrict its application to land. The use of sewage sludge on land is now strictly controlled by EC Directive 86/278. This directive provides two alternative means of controlling sludge application to land. One method is to state the maximum quantities of sludge (as tonnes dry matter) that can be added to a unit area of soil each year, while at the same time staying within the limits set for heavy metals in the sludge. The second method is to use the limit value quoted for the amount of heavy metals which may be added annually to agricultural land, based on a ten-year average. It is the second method which has been adopted in the UK.

The disposal of sewage sludge would be greatly facilitated if the concentration of heavy metals in it could be reduced. This could be achieved by strict trade effluent control. This approach is now being pursued more vigorously not only for inorganic pollutants but also for some organic pollutants.

Dumping at sea

At present, sludge (from London, Manchester, Strathclyde and Belfast, for example) is transported in purpose-built vessels and dumped at sea, usually outside the three-mile limit. The sludge is dumped while the vessels are moving and care is taken to ensure that the solids are in a finely divided form and the point of discharge is such that material is not washed back on to the beaches. In some instances (e.g. that of Strathclyde), the sludge is dumped into a deep trench in the sea bed so that the area affected is very limited.

This method might appear to be acceptable as the sludge will be diluted and might be broken down by the natural processes which take place in the marine environment. However, the dumping areas suffer severe damage because of local overloading. The volumes of sludge are too great to be dispersed and broken down rapidly enough.

At present, the disposal of wastes at sea is controlled by the Dumping at Sea Act 1974, which prohibits disposal without a licence, and is monitored by the Ministry of Agriculture, Fisheries and Food.

The future of sludge dumping at sea, however, is limited as the UK has agreed, in line with the decisions taken at the Third North Sea Conference of 1990, to stop all sea disposal of sludge by 1998. This will create a considerable problem as, with the tighter controls on sludge application to land, attention is now being focused on the costly possibility of incineration.

Incineration

Incineration will destroy any toxic organic compounds present in the sludge and leave the toxic metals unaffected (except those which are volatile) in the non-combustible ash, which is inert. The main gain in incineration is the large reduction in the volume of waste to be disposed of, along with the elimination of the nuisance from biological decomposition. Incineration still leaves the ash (some 25–40% of the incoming load on a dry basis) to be disposed of and this can have high polluting qualities. The gaseous effluent from the incinerator will also have to meet the required standards, and this is discussed in Units 14–16. Even with all these considerations, incineration is seen by many as the most practicable alternative to sea dumping of sewage sludge. In some instances sewage sludge has been incinerated along with domestic refuse or coal slurry.

Other current methods of sludge disposal include:

1   dumping in large sludge lagoons or sludge beds;

2   dumping in trenches which are then filled in with soil;

3   composting with household refuse to form an organic manure;

4   dumping of dewatered and dried sludge on selected landfill sites.

The first method can cause objectionable smells because the sludge dries slowly. Method 3 does not receive much favour since the resulting manure often contains broken glass and other debris, and it is unsuitable if the sludge contains toxic wastes such as heavy metals. In the fourth method the quality of the material to be discharged with regard to smell, groundwater pollution, and space and transport requirements, is of crucial importance. Where the quality is acceptable, method 4 is not likely to add significantly to the problems already arising from the presence of refuse.

It is worth noting that all the methods considered depend on the availability of land.

SAQ 32

Which treatment processes give rise to sludge?

SAQ 33

(a)   What volume of sludge is produced per day from a sewage treatment works with primary sedimentation and a low-rate biological filter which serves a town of 100 000 population? Take the sludge density as 1000 kg m^{-3}.

(b)   What volume will be produced from primary sedimentation with an activated sludge process?

SAQ 34

What are some of the benefits of treating sludge by anaerobic digestion?

6.5   Summary

In a sewage treatment works, the main sidestream products, apart from screenings and grit, are the various forms of sludge, comprising the underflow from primary and secondary sedimentation tanks. Treatment and disposal of these sludges depends on the volume and characteristics of the sludges produced.

The treatment and disposal of sludges is sometimes considered an unimportant additional operation added to the end of a wastewater treatment system. In fact, sludge treatment usually represents the largest proportion of the total cost of sewage treatment. It is therefore important to consider sludge treatment and disposal costs as part of the overall economics of a treatment plant. High-rate biological processes can reduce the size of secondary treatment plant but bring with them additional loadings in sludge treatment.

The decanted waterflow from sludge dewatering represents a significant load of recycled suspended solids and BOD to the treatment works. The effects of the final disposal methods and return flows from sludge treatment can have major implications. This is the reason for regarding sewage treatment as a separation process producing a low-solids stream (treated effluent) and a high-solids stream (sludge).

Sludge treatment and disposal is a considerable problem. Methods of treatment include thickening with mechanical dewatering, air drying, and anaerobic digestion. Methods of disposal currently used include land application, burial in trenches or landfill sites, sea dumping (to cease by the end of 1998) and incineration.

7   INDUSTRIAL EFFLUENTS

7.1   Introduction

Industrial effluents (usually called 'trade effluents' or 'trade wastes' in the UK) come from a variety of manufacturing processes such as those producing textiles, metals, food and dairy products. They usually have a wider range of characteristics than domestic sewage and are more likely to contain toxic and non-biodegradable compounds that require physico-chemical treatment rather than biological oxidation. Treatment usually takes place in a series of unit operations designed to remove or to modify the characteristics of the pollutants in the effluent. There are many trade wastes, however, which can be biodegraded, provided any toxic components present are first removed. This is usually achieved using chemical treatment, e.g. oxidation of high concentrations of cyanides.

7.2   Treatment of industrial effluents

It can often be advantageous to treat industrial effluents in admixture with domestic sewage: for instance, the final composition of the mixed effluent stream may achieve the BOD:N:P ratio of 100:5:1 required for biotreatment. There can also be significant savings in capital and operating costs as one plant (instead of many) would suffice. So in many cities, industrial effluents (especially from the smaller industries) are discharged into the sewer system, after pretreatment where necessary. The industry concerned pays a charge to the authority responsible for the sewers and the receiving treatment plant. The magnitude of the fee (as discussed in Units 5–6) depends on the polluting potential of the effluent (based on the COD), its suspended solids content and the volumetric flow rate. The receiving authority dictates what can be put into the sewers by issuing a consent to discharge limiting the value of these three parameters and the content of any components of concern (e.g. metals) that may affect the biotreatment process. The toxic content of trade effluent discharged into sewers also has to be controlled in order to safeguard men working on sewers and to protect the piping and equipment in the sewerage system from chemical attack.

 Typical pretreatment operations carried out on industrial effluents prior to despatch to a sewage treatment plant include the following (also see the entry for ***effluent, physico-chemical treatment*** in the set book):

1   solids removal, e.g. by screening, sedimentation, filtration or microstraining;

2   pH adjustment, using acid or alkali to bring the waste water to a pH value in the range 6.5–8.0;

3   chemical oxidation, e.g. oxidation of the highly toxic cyanide (CN^-) ion to the much less toxic cyanate (CNO^-) ion;

4   chemical reduction, e.g. reduction of the toxic Cr^{6+} ion to the Cr^{3+} ion using SO_2;

5   removal/recovery of heavy metals, e.g. precipitation of Cd using lime;

6   oil/fat/grease removal, e.g. using an oil ***interceptor*** (Figure 52) or by flotation;

7   trace organics removal, e.g. adsorption of pesticides using activated carbon.

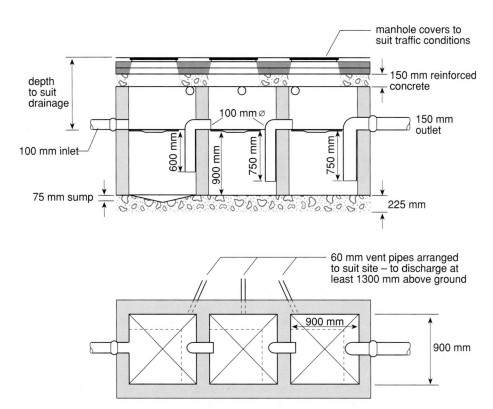

Figure 52 *Plan and section of an oil interceptor – the retention time is sufficient for any oil to rise to the surface from where it is removed during periodic inspections. (All dimensions are in millimetres.)*

While most industrial effluents are dealt with efficiently and inconspicuously, mishaps can occur, often on a massive scale. In January 1992 millions of gallons of waste water containing the metals arsenic, mercury, cadmium, iron, zinc and copper poured from the disused Wheal Jane tin mine into the Fal estuary in Cornwall (Figure 53). The estuary was turned from an enticing blue (before the incident) to bright orange. Not only was tourism affected but also concern was raised regarding the integrity of the quality of water in boreholes supplying the area. The quality of oysters and other shellfish in the estuary also came under scrutiny. Immediate remedial measures taken to reduce the input of heavy metals into the estuary included dosing the effluent with lime to bring about precipitation of the metals, followed by sedimentation.

7.3 Pulp production for the paper industry

As an example of an industrial process requiring effluent treatment let us consider paper-making. This requires pulp which is obtained from timber, although recycled fibres from old newspapers and magazines are increasingly used as a substitute.

Television broadcast TV4 shows how a typical pulp manufacturing plant operates. The programme also features the effluent treatment system needed to deal with the waste water produced in this activity.

Figure 54 shows in schematic form the process operations used to produce pulp from logs. At the paper mill featured in the television programme, sitka spruce is the predominant species of timber used. Apart from its widespread availability in the UK, it gives a pulp with high strength and brightness, which are essential for high-quality newsprint.

The spruce logs are first debarked in a revolving drum where the abrasive action of the logs rubbing against each other removes the bark. The bark is conveyed to a fluidised bed bark boiler where it is burnt to produce energy with which steam is generated. (The steam is used to dry the paper produced much later in the process.)

Toxic metal leak poisons water supply

By Paul Stokes

TOXIC material leaking from a redundant Cornish tin mine was yesterday creating severe pollution and threatening an environmental catastrophe.

Millions of gallons of rust-coloured water are discharging from a maze of disused workings near the recently abandoned Wheal Jane mine, near Truro, into the Fal estuary and nearby Mylor and Restronguet creeks in west Cornwall.

Several miles of the River Carnon have been severely discoloured by the foaming discharge and there is concern that the "acid water" could get into the food chain.

It contains metals, including arsenic, cadmium, iron, zinc and copper, and caused a reaction when it came into contact with the sea water.

Households supplied with water from boreholes have been told to use bottled water, oysters caught locally were being tested for metal poisoning and bathers have been warned against using the affected rivers and creeks.

The water has been seeping out for several months, but on Monday there was a huge surge with up to 10 million gallons of highly contaminated liquid being released from an undergound shaft.

By last night the flow had reduced and the quality improved, although millions of gallons were still discharging.

The National Rivers Authority faces a multi-million pound bill to find a solu-

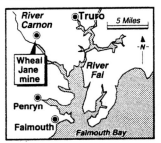

tion to the complex problem. If the flow is stopped in one direction it will come out in another among the warren of connected old workings.

It is believed the discharge may contain the highest levels of heavy metals in any British pollution incident.

Preliminary tests show levels of cadmium 100 times higher than the accepted European Community standard. The levels of zinc in some areas of the river are also nine times the accepted standard.

Mr Roger Hamilton, the NRA's regional environmental scientist, said a possible short term solution was for pumping work to be recommenced at Wheal Jane, which closed in March 1991.

"There is a possibility that contamination from Wheal Jane could seep out for a century or more." he said.

Mr Matthew Taylor. MP for Truro, described it as the biggest pollution incident of its kind in Europe.

He said: "I warned Ministers earlier this would be the consequence and the evidence is now there for all to see."

Figure 53   *The story of the Wheal Jane tin mine (from* The Daily Telegraph, *17 January 1992).*

The debarked logs are then chipped. The chips are washed and then processed in a refiner, where they are steam-heated (to soften them) and then broken down to fine fibres by a system of static and rotating discs. This type of refining is called thermo-mechanical pulping (TMP). In the refiner the cellulose fibres are separated from the lignin which is present in the wood. The fibres are screened and any coarse fibres are refined further. The pulp is then thickened, bleached with sodium hydrosulphite ($Na_2S_2O_4$) and sent on to the paper mill. Effluent is generated largely in the chip washer.

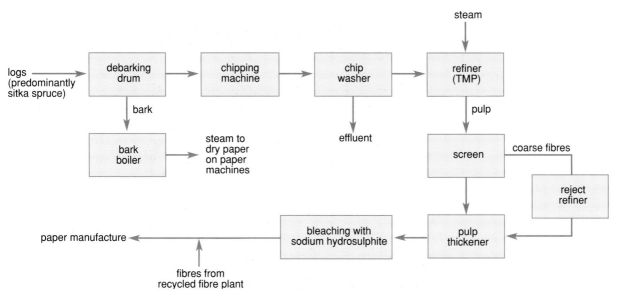

Figure 54 *Flow diagram of pulp manufacturing process.*

As mentioned above, recycled fibres are used in the plant. The processing of old newspapers and magazines is also complex (Figure 55). The materials are pulped with chemicals, then screened, and put into a chest or holding tank where the chemicals (e.g. hydrogen peroxide) react fully. Cleaning and screening then takes place to remove items such as staples. Flotation is used to de-ink the pulp. Fine cleaning and screening occurs, followed by pulp dewatering using a disc filter and wire press. The

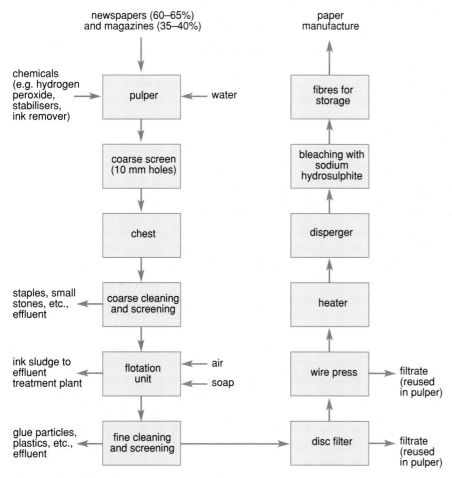

Figure 55 *Flow diagram of recycled fibre plant.*

pulp is then heated and broken into fine fibres using a disperger, consisting of two circular plates with rows of teeth facing each other – one plate stays stationary while the other revolves at high speed. The pulp passes between the two plates (1–2 mm) apart and the pulp particles are reduced in size. The final product is bleached again (this time with sodium hydrosulphite) and stored for use later on the paper machines. Effluent in the recycled fibre plant is generated in the cleaning processes and in the de-inking system. There is reuse of some of the effluent from the process – the waste waters from the disc filters are reused in the pulper.

7.4   Effluent treatment in the pulp production process

The combined effluents from the pulp manufacturing process are passed through a primary clarifier (Figure 56) where suspended solids (mainly fibres) settle out. These are dewatered in a sludge press and then burnt in the bark boiler. The supernatant from the clarifier goes into an activated sludge unit for biological treatment.

The effluents from the recycled fibre plant go through a flotation unit where solids are separated out to be dewatered later by a centrifuge. These solids are also burnt in the bark boiler. The effluent from the flotation unit goes to the activated sludge tank which has a retention time of about 36 hours for effluents from both the pulp plant and the recycled fibre process. The activated sludge unit is followed by a secondary clarifier in which the biomass from the biological treatment stage settles out. Most of this sludge (90–95%) is recycled to the activated sludge tank. The remaining sludge is

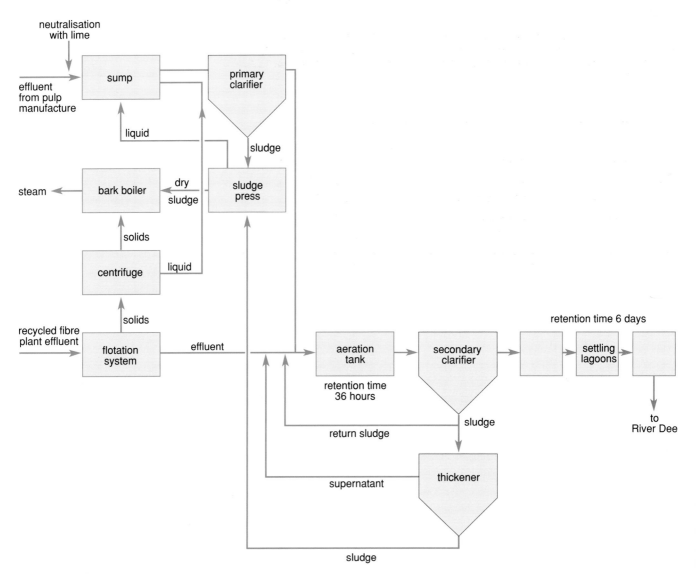

Figure 56   *Flow diagram of effluent treatment at the paper mill.*

thickened, pressed and then incinerated (in the bark boiler). The sludge from the biological stage contains heavy metals from the printing inks from the recycled fibre plant. These make it difficult to dispose of the sludge by landfarming or landfill, and incineration is the preferred option. For similar reasons, the solids centrifuged from the recycled fibre plant effluent are also incinerated. The fly ash produced through incineration contains the heavy metals and is sent to an appropriately licensed site for disposal.

The outflow from the secondary clarifier goes through three settling lagoons where over six days more solids settle out. At the exit of the final lagoon the values of BOD and suspended solids in the treated effluent are about 15 g m^{-3} and 25 g m^{-3} respectively. These values satisfy the consent conditions for discharge to the nearby River Dee.

7.5 Summary

Industrial effluents generally have a wider range of wastewater characteristics than domestic sewage and may contain toxic and refractory components. With appropriate pretreatment, industrial effluents may often be treated together with domestic sewage, resulting in cost savings and more effective control of pollution. In situations where the volume and/or the pollution load of the industrial effluent is high it has to be treated on its own.

SAQ 35

Table 10 lists industrial and manufacturing activities (Column I), pollutants (Column II) and pretreatment options (Column III). For each activity, select the pollutant you would expect to find and the pretreatment operation necessary before the effluent can be discharged into a domestic sewer.

Table 10

Column I	Column II	Column III
Ceramic works	oil and fat	chemical reduction
Distillery	chromium VI	neutralisation
Chicken processing plant	acidic mine waters	sedimentation
Electroplating works	china clay	microstraining
Copper mining	spent grain	flotation

Reference

PORTEOUS, A. (1992) *Dictionary of Environmental Science and Technology*, John Wiley & Sons (T237 set book).

Acknowledgements

Grateful acknowledgement is made to the following sources for permission to reproduce material in this unit.

Figures

Cover illustration: based on an original by Ian Howatson, courtesy of Ian Howatson Illustration, Buckingham; *cover photograph:* Howard Humphreys and Sons; *Figures 1, 3, 8, 10, 12, 13, 19:* courtesy of Howard Humphreys Consulting Engineers; *Figures 11, 28, 29:* Burberry, P. (1992) *Environment and Services: Mitchell's Building Series*, Longman Group UK Ltd; *Figures 16, 17:* Hall, T. and Hÿde, R.A. (1992) *Water Treatment, Processes and Practices*, WRC Swindon; *Figures 21, 25, 39b:* adapted from Sundstrom, D.W. and Klei, H.E. (1979) *Waste Water Treatment*, Prentice-Hall Inc, © Donald W. Sundstrom and Herbert E. Klei 1979; *Figures 22, 51:* Metcalf and Eddy Inc, revised by Tchobanoglous, G. (1987) *Wastewater Engineering: Treatment, Disposal, Reuse*, McGraw-Hill Inc; *Figure 23:* Morrey, C. (1991) *Digest of Environmental Protection and Water Statistics*, Department of the Environment/HMSO; *Figures 24, 26, 27:* adapted from Overman, M. (1968) *Water*, Aldus Books Ltd; *Figure 33:* Jones & Attwood Ltd; *Figure 34:* from *Unit Processes: Primary Sedimentation*, courtesy of the Institution of Water and Environmental Management; *Figure 36:* courtesy of Biwater Treatment Ltd; *Figure 37:* courtesy of the Water Research Centre, Marlow, Bucks; *Figure 40:* aerator redrawn from information supplied by Simon-Hartley Limited; *Figure 43:* adapted from the *Whitehead and Poole Oxidation Ditch System Brochure*, courtesy of Biwater Europe Ltd; *Figure 44:* reproduced with the kind permission of Wimpey Construction Ltd; *Figure 45:* from the *ICI Brochure – The ICI Deep Shaft Process*, courtesy of ICI Biological Products; *Figure 46:* courtesy of Farrer Sewage Ltd; *Figure 48:* from *The Chemical Engineer*, 14 March 1991, courtesy of the Institution of Chemical Engineers; *Figure 49: British Standards Code of Practice for Design and Installation of Small Sewage Treatment Works and Cesspools, BS6297:1983*, courtesy of BSI; *Figure 53:* Stokes, P. (1992) 'Toxic metal leak poisons water supply', *Daily Telegraph*, 17 January 1992, © The Daily Telegraph plc, 1992.

Tables

Table 2: from *Waterfacts 1991*, courtesy of the Water Services Association; *Table 3:* Nace, R.L. (1967) 'World water inventory and control', in Chorley, R.J. (ed.), *Water, Earth and Man*, Methuen and Co Ltd; *Table 7:* Metcalf and Eddy Inc, revised by Tchobanoglous, G. (1987) *Wastewater Engineering: Treatment, Disposal, Re-Use*, 2nd edition, McGraw-Hill Inc; *Table 8: Health Guidelines for the Use of Wastewater in Agriculture and Aquaculture: Report of a WHO Scientific Group*, Geneva, World Health Organization, 1989, (WHO Technical Report Series, No 778), table 3, p 39.